A CIVIL WAR JOURNAL

A
CIVIL WAR
JOURNAL

A Collection of Little-Known Facts and Other Odds-and-Ends about the Civil War

Compiled by
Albert A. Nofi

GALAHAD BOOKS
New York

First Promontory Press edition published in 1995.

Promontory Press
A division of Budget Book Service, Inc.
386 Park Avenue South
New York, NY 10016

Promontory Press is a registered trademark of Budget Book Service, Inc.

Published by arrangement with Combined Books, Inc.

Library of Congress Catalog Card Number: 95-067048

ISBN: 0-88394-090-6

Printed in the United States of America.

CONTENTS

Before the War

*T*he room in which Robert E. Lee was born seems to have also been the birthplace of two signers of the Declaration of Independence, his uncles Richard Henry Lee and Francis Lightfoot Lee.

★ ★ ★

*D*uring the election of 1860, Northern voters cast a quarter of a million more votes against Lincoln than did the entire South.

★ ★ ★

*T*he first African slaves landed in Virginia on the shores of what became the United States in 1619.

★ ★ ★

*A*t West Point in the decades before the war, it was customary for cadets who were indulging in a little illicit alcohol to turn their backs when imbibing, so that their classmates could honestly testify that they had not witnessed a fellow cadet drinking.

★ ★ ★

*O*nly 3 percent of all firearms made in the United States in 1860 were produced in the South.

★ ★ ★

*I*n the spring of 1848 several American officers toured various natural wonders in central Mexico, including a vast cavern in which they almost got lost—possibly forever—which would surely have had a significant effect on the Civil War, for the party included the future Union generals U.S. Grant, Andrew Porter, Charles P. Stone and Zealous B. Tower, and the future Confederate generals Richard Anderson, Henry H. Sibley, George Crittenden, Simon B. Buckner and Mansfield Lovell.

★ ★ ★

*I*n 1836 Lt. Robert Anderson's star pupil in artillery tactics at West Point was Cadet Pierre G.T. Beauregard, who considered Anderson his favorite instructor and who, 25 years later, directed the bombardment of Ft. Sumter, which Anderson commanded.

★ ★ ★

*T*he first state to abolish slavery was Rhode Island, which did so in 1774, two years before the Declaration of Independence.

★　★　★

*C*adet Philip Sheridan was supposed to graduate from West Point in 1852, but was suspended for a year for a "quarrel of a belligerent character," having used a bayonet on Cadet William R. Terrill, who later died at Perryville as a Union brigadier general.

★　★　★

*O*n 27 June 1860, Maj. Albert J. Myer, who was by training a surgeon, was appointed chief signal officer of the United States Army, and thus head of the first independent Signal Corps in history, which consisted of precisely one man, himself.

★　★　★

*D*uring the Mexican War, Capt. Robert E. Lee was almost killed by an over-zealous sentry, escaping with but a singed uniform.

★　★　★

*I*n 1836 Cadet Lewis A. Armistead, who died leading a brigade in Pickett's Charge at Gettysburg, was expelled from West Point for breaking a dinner plate over the head of Jubal A. Early, who rose to command a corps in the Confederate Army.

★　★　★

During the 1850s both Charles K. Graham and George S. Greene, who later led Union brigades at Gettysburg and on other fields, were employed as engineers in the design and construction of New York's Central Park.

A highly dubious tradition credits Abner Doubleday, who rose to become a Union major general, with the invention of baseball in 1839, when he was just 19 and a cadet at West Point.

★ ★ ★

The first American to gain the ramparts of Chapultepec Castle on 13 September 1847, against the heroic resistance of the cadets of the Mexican military academy, was Lt. George E. Pickett, who, almost 16 years later, failed in an attempt to storm Cemetery Ridge at Gettysburg.

★ ★ ★

In 1842 future Union Brig. Gen. Joseph Andrew Jackson Lightburn attempted to secure an appointment to West Point, only to be passed over in favor of future Confederate Lt. Gen. Thomas J. Jackson, the "Gallant Stonewall."

*I*n 1482 Pope Pius II roundly condemned the slave trade, a measure which had to be repeated by Pope Paul III in 1557, Urban VIII in 1639, Benedict XIV in 1741 and Gregory XVI in 1839.

*G*eorge B. McClellan, who was something of a child prodigy, had to secure special permission of the secretary of war to be admitted to West Point in 1842, since he was only 15 years old.

*T*he first astronomical observatory in the United States, the Cincinnati Observatory, was established in 1845, largely through the efforts of Ormsby MacKnight Mitchel, a West Point classmate of Robert E. Lee and Joseph E. Johnston, who became a Union major general during the war and died of yellow fever in 1862.

*I*n his four years at West Point, Cadet U.S. Grant is said to have never attended a single dance.

*W*hile conducting a survey of Barataria Bay, Louisiana, in 1840, Lt. Pierre G.T. Beauregard supervised an estimated 10,000 soundings.

*F*or some years before the Civil War Ambrose P. Hill courted one Ellen Marcy, who jilted him and in 1860 married his erstwhile West Point roommate, George B. McClellan, a fact to which the troops later attributed Hill's singular aggressiveness against his successful rival, so that during one attack a Union veteran was heard to cry, "My God, Nellie, why didn't you marry him?"

★ ★ ★

*I*n 1860 the South produced only 4 percent of all locomotives made in the United States.

★ ★ ★

*J*ames J. Pettigrew, who died a Confederate brigadier general during the Gettysburg campaign, graduated from the University of North Carolina in 1847 with such high distinction in mathematics that he was immediately appointed a professor of the subject at the United States Naval Observatory.

*S*ince a free black was at risk of being kidnapped by slave catchers, relatively prominent and prosperous freedmen in the South often preferred to own their wives and offspring and even parents, rather than liberate them.

★ ★ ★

*W*illiam Tecumseh Sherman was considered the best chef in his class at West Point, cooking an excellent hash over the fireplace in his room, an activity which was strictly against the rules.

★ ★ ★

*N*ot long before the Civil War broke out the heavily Irish *69th New York* refused to parade in honor of Mr. Charles Renfrew—the Prince of Wales traveling incognito—leading the State Adjutant General to charge the entire regiment with mutiny, charges which were still pending in April of 1861, when they were dropped so that the regiment could march off to war.

★ ★ ★

*W*hen Louis M. Goldsborough entered the United States Navy in 1817 at the age of eleven, as was then the custom, family connections—his father was chief clerk of the Navy Department—managed to get his warrant as midshipman predated to 1812, so that he gained five years seniority, which meant he was a naval officer from the age of six.

★ ★ ★

*A*t a "commercial convention" in 1859, representatives of most of the Southern states resolved that the African slave trade should be reopened, a measure which was enthusiastically endorsed by a delegate from Mississippi named Jefferson F. Davis.

★ ★ ★

*W*hen Ulysses S. Grant married Julia Dent on 22 August 1848, the best man was James Longstreet.

★ ★ ★

*O*n the eve of the Civil War the United States Army had 183 of its 198 companies (92.4 percent) west of the Mississippi, or, to put it another way, one soldier for every 120 square miles west of the "Father of the Waters," and one for every 1,300 square miles east of it.

★ ★ ★

*T*homas W. Sherman, who eventually rose to a brigadier generalcy in the Union Army, secured an appointment to West Point in 1832 by asking President Andrew Jackson for it after having walked to Washington from his native Rhode Island.

★ ★ ★

*I*n 1855 the North Carolina legislature declared that the Melungeon Indians were descendants of the "Lost Colony of Roanoke" and therefore eligible to marry whites, while the Tennessee legislature declared that they were "persons of color" and prohibited from marrying whites.

*T*he total "value" of slaves in the United States in 1860 was approximately $2 billion, or an average of about $500 for each man, woman and child held in bondage.

*A*s a young man, William T. Sherman disliked his red hair so much he once attempted to dye it, only to make matters worse, for it turned "an odd shade of green."

*S*ome years before the war Pierre G.T. Beauregard was briefly under arrest for participating in a duel with shotguns.

*P*ublished in 1852, Harriet Beecher Stowe's *Uncle Tom's Cabin* sold 300,000 copies in its first year in print, and another 100,000 over the following six months.

*A*braham Lincoln was born on 12 February 1809, near Hogdenville, Kentucky, less than 100 miles from where Jefferson Davis had been born in Christian County, Kentucky, nine months earlier, on 3 June 1808.

★ ★ ★

*B*etween 1802 and 1860, 1,875 men graduated from West Point, of whom about 85 percent were still alive at the outbreak of the Civil War, and about 1,100 (58.7 percent) saw service.

★ ★ ★

*F*ragments of the gallows on which John Brown was hanged were sold as souvenirs for $1 apiece, a good day's wage for a common laborer in 1859.

★ ★ ★

*T*he Sibley tent, an elaborate teepee-like affair for up to 20 men designed before the war by Maj. Henry Hopkins Sibley, later a Confederate general, had one drawback: the stove issued for it had a chimney too short to reach the opening from whence it was supposed to emerge, so that the tent rapidly filled with smoke, which may help explain why it saw little use during the war.

★ ★ ★

*W*ade Hampton, who later became one of the South's finest cavalrymen, was probably the largest slaveholder in the country, with some 3,500 human beings numbered among his chattels.

*A*s a result of an accidental wound to the knee in 1839, Lt. Lucius B. Northrop went on "indefinite" sick leave from the army until January of 1861, whereupon his health recovered sufficiently for his friend Jefferson Davis to name him Commissary General of the Confederacy, a post in which he was highly incompetent.

*I*nvited to drill his hometown militia company while on graduation leave from West Point in the summer of 1846, the newly minted 2nd Lt. Thomas J. Jackson bungled the job so badly that he marched the men off the parade ground and right out of town.

*T*he Richmond Howitzers, a Virginia militia company which would prove a tough outfit in the coming war, once buried a pet crow in an elaborate military ceremony which included two eulogies in English plus an oration in Latin and an ode in Greek.

*A*t the time of the Civil War an estimated 25 percent of Southern whites had at least one black ancestor.

★ ★ ★

*I*n a period of 31 months from 1842 to 1845, the Corps of Engineers removed from the Lower Ohio, the Mississippi, the Missouri and the Arkansas Rivers 133,331 obstacles to navigation, including 21,681 snags, 36,840 roots, logs and stumps, and 74,810 trees.

★ ★ ★

*A*ccording to a tradition of dubious provenance, while a cadet at West Point, Pierre G.T. Beauregard had a romance with Virginia Scott, daughter of Winfield Scott, the most distinguished officer in the army, who, when her family broke off the affair, entered a convent, where she died in 1845.

★ ★ ★

*W*hen still a teenager Jesse Grant, father of Ulysses, lived for a time with the family of John Brown.

★ ★ ★

*B*etween 1619 and 1865 an estimated 500,000 kidnapped Africans were sold into slavery in the United States.

★ ★ ★

*I*n 1859 Barton Key, son of Francis Scott "The Star Spangled Banner" Key, was killed by an outraged husband, Tammany politician, and future Union general, Daniel Sickles, who was acquitted by reason of temporary insanity, the first time such a plea had ever been made.

*T*he two most vehemently secessionist states, South Carolina and Mississippi, were also the only states in which black slaves constituted a majority of the population, 57.2 percent in the former and 55.2 percent in the latter.

*L*incoln began to grow his famous beard shortly after the Election of 1860, primarily at the urging of eleven year old Grace Bedell of Westfield, N.Y., who, on 18 October had written ". . . you would look a great deal better for your face is so thin."

*O*f the approximately one million white families in the South, over a third, some 385,000, owned at least one of the 3,953,760 slaves in the region in 1860, for an average of 10.26 slaves per family, though in fact most slaveholding families had only one or two slaves: about 100,000 families had 10 or more slaves, 46,279 had at least 20 slaves, about 10,000 had at least 50 and 2,292 had at least 100.

*W*hen John Brown was hanged at Charlestown, Virginia, on 2 December 1859, one of the Virginia militiamen present was Pvt. John Wilkes Booth.

★ ★ ★

A number of men who became prominent in the Civil War had soldiered for the Republic of Texas: Gen. Albert Sidney Johnston, who went to Texas after the Revolution and served for a time as commanding officer of the Texas Army, Maj. Gen. George B. Crittenden and brigadier generals Thomas Green, Joseph L. Hogg, Jerome Bonaparte Robertson, Ben McCulloch and Thomas Green, Confederates all.

★ ★ ★

*I*n a demonstration of the gallantry, honor, courage, nobility and gentility of Southern manhood, on 22 May 1856 Sen. Charles Sumner of Massachusetts was beaten into unconsciousness while sitting at his desk in the Senate by Rep. Preston Smith Brooks of South Carolina, who objected to a speech in which Sumner had denounced Brooks' uncle, Andrew P. Butler, as a servant of "the harlot Slavery."

★ ★ ★

On the basis of photographs some medical experts have concluded that Abraham Lincoln suffered from Marfan's Syndrome, a collagen disorder which, among other things, causes long, thin bones and a shortened lifespan.

★　★　★

The first ironclad warship in the United States Navy was the so-called *Stevens Ram,* which, though authorized in 1842 and actually begun in 1854, was never completed and was scrapped on the stocks in 1874.

★　★　★

So effective was the military government of Winfield Scott during the American occupation of Mexico in 1848 that, upon conclusion of the peace treaty, some residents urged the *gringogeneral* to stay behind and become president of Mexico.

★　★　★

In order to get a closer look at the execution of John Brown, secessionist fanatic Edmund Ruffin donned a Virginia Military Institute uniform and marched two miles, shouldering a musket in the ranks of boys young enough to be his grandsons.

★　★　★

In the twenty years preceding the Civil War it is estimated that some 15,000 slaves succeeded in escaping to freedom.

A number of other men who later rose to some importance in the Civil War took part in the Black Hawk War of 1832: Abraham Lincoln, the Confederacy's Gen. Albert Sidney Johnston and Maj. Gen. George R. Crittenden were infantry officers. Robert Anderson, the defender of Fort Sumter, who rose to become a Union major general, served as a colonel of Illinois volunteers; John A. McClernand, who became a Union major general, served as a militiaman; while Edwin Vose Sumner, later an able Union major general, and Philip St. George Cook, later a Union brigadier general, served as officers in the Regular Army.

1861

The first man killed in the Civil War was Pvt. Daniel Hough [Huff] of *Company E, 1st Artillery*, who died as a result of the premature discharge of a cannon being used to fire a salute during evacuation ceremonies after the surrender of Fort Sumter on 14 April 1861.

★ ★ ★

On 3 May 1861 the Congress of the Confederate States of America declared war on the United States of America.

★ ★ ★

*D*uring the West Virginia campaign in mid-1861, a company of green Illinois volunteers was wearily making its way down a road in execrable marching order until its captain shouted, "Close up, boys! Damn you, close up! If the enemy were to fire on you when you're straggling along that way, they couldn't hit a damn one of you! Close up!" Whereupon the troops closed up.

★ ★ ★

*I*n January of 1861 Southern sympathizers in California attempted to establish a "Pacific Republic" by an uprising at Stockton, which was rapidly overcome by loyal citizens.

★ ★ ★

*P*ierre G.T. Beauregard had the shortest tenure of any superintendent of West Point, from 23 to 28 January 1861, when he was dismissed for seditious behavior.

★ ★ ★

*W*hen the Rev. William N. Pendleton (West Point, '30), who eventually became a brigadier general in the Confederate Army, took command of a battery in 1861 he promptly named the guns "Matthew," "Mark," "Luke" and "John."

★ ★ ★

*F*or several weeks early in the war Mrs. Robert E. Lee continued to live at Arlington, the family home, despite the fact that Union Maj. Gen. Irvin McDowell had made it his headquarters.

*D*rill instructors were in such short supply at the onset of the war that 13-year-old cadets from places such as Virginia Military Institute were pressed into service to drill men old enough to be their fathers and grandfathers.

*W*hen a brave Texan rode out to retrieve a flag which had fallen between the lines at the battle of Wilson's Creek (10 August 1861), the men of the Union *1st Iowa* held their fire, calling out to the troops on either side to likewise honor a gallant enemy.

*O*ne night late in 1861 pickets of the *3rd New York Artillery* took into custody three men in a coach who were proceeding suspiciously through one of the army camps about Washington, only to discover to their dismay that they had arrested the president, the secretary of state and the commander of the *Army of the Potomac.*

*T*he Meagher Guards of Charleston, composed of Irish volunteers for the Confederacy, became the Emerald Light Infantry shortly after Sumter fell, when it was learned that Irish nationalist hero Thomas F. Meagher [Marr], after whom the company was named, had raised a company for the Yankee *69th New York*.

★ ★ ★

*T*he first naval officer to be killed in action was Cdr. James H. Ward, U.S.N., who died on 27 June 1861, while leading an effort to dislodge some Confederate batteries covering the lower Potomac from Mathias Point, Virginia.

★ ★ ★

*S*hortly after the battle of Belmont (7 November 1861), Yankee Brig. Gen. U.S. Grant and Rebel Brig. Cen. Benjamin F. Cheatham met on a riverboat to negotiate certain technical matters relative to the exchange of prisoners and similar formalities, during which they fell into a discussion of horseflesh, whereupon Cheatham challenged Grant to a race to decide the war, which the latter, noted for his equestrian ability, declined.

★ ★ ★

*C*onfederate Brig. Gen. Frank C. Armstrong began his Civil War service as a lieutenant in the Union *2nd Cavalry* at the first battle of Bull Run, not resigning to "go South" until 13 August 1861, by which time the war was well under way.

★ ★ ★

*A*lthough the *7th New York Militia* was one of the first Federal regiments to reach Washington, it suffered not a single battle death in its 150 days of service during three separate wartime enlistments. But of the 991 men on the rolls in April of 1861 fully 603 (60.9 percent) went on to become officers in other regiments, 58 dying in the service.

★ ★ ★

*D*uring the first winter of the war, patriotic Quaker ladies in Pennsylvania attempted to do something for the boys in blue by providing some "non-lethal" supplies in the form of mittens, which, alas, were of only marginal use since the good ladies refrained from putting trigger fingers on them.

★ ★ ★

*T*he first Regular Army officer to die in the war was Lt. J. T. Greble of the *2nd Artillery,* who fell by his guns at Big Bethel on 10 June 1861, which was also the occasion of the first nonfatal wound to be received by a Regular Army officer, Capt. Hugh Judson Kilpatrick of the *5th New York,* who later became a major general of volunteers.

*N*o one knows whether it was a Yank or a Reb who made one of the most monumental discoveries of the war, but the troops of both sides very quickly learned that the barrel of a musket could hold nearly a pint of whiskey.

*I*n a letter dated 29 March 1861, Abraham Lincoln, president of the world's greatest and most troubled republic, was informed by Regent Captain Gaetano Bellurri that he had been elected an honorary citizen of the world's smallest and oldest republic, San Marino.

*A*ccording to Article 2, Paragraph 5, of the Confederate Atmy regulations, if two officers of the same rank had the same date of commission and no prior United States or Confederate military service, questions of seniority were to be decided by a lottery.

★ ★ ★

The largest warships under construction in America in 1861 were the 5,610 ton broadside ironclads *Re d'Italia* and *Re di Portogallo,* laid down at the Webb shipyard in New York in November and December of that year under contract from the Royal Italian Navy.

★ ★ ★

Allan Pinkerton, head of intelligence for the *Army of the Potomac, is* said to have evaluated the suitability of women to serve as agents by means of phrenology.

★ ★ ★

Long after he had accepted a brigadier generalcy in the Confederate Army and while he was commanding Confederate forces facing Ft. Sumter—Pierre G.T. Beauregard was still dunning the United States Army for travel expenses incurred pursuant to his final transfer shortly before he resigned to "go South."

★ ★ ★

Slaves constituted 25 percent or more of the population of each of the states which seceded from the Union.

★ ★ ★

*T*o provide for the enormous number of troops in Washington in the early months of the war a huge bakery was installed under the west front terrace of the Capitol where 16,000 loaves of bread were baked each day in mid-1861.

★　★　★

*W*hile riding in the Shenandoah Valley one day in December of 1861, Thomas "Stonewall" Jackson espied a persimmon tree ladened with fruit, whereupon he halted his staff, climbed up into the branches and ate his fill.

★　★　★

*W*hen some Southern militia regiments went to war in 1861 the "gentlemen privates" were accompanied by their slave menservants, often wearing the same uniforms as their masters; the 3rd Alabama marched off with about a thousand white rank and file plus "several hundred" black servants.

★　★　★

*E*benezer W. Peirce, a brigadier general of New York militia, was so remorseful about bungling the "battle" of Big Bethel, Virginia, on 10 June 1861, that he shortly afterwards resigned his militia commission and reenlisted as a private, in which capacity he served until discharged three years later.

★　★　★

*W*hen Federal troops occupied Arlington, most of the furnishings and household goods of the Lee family were rescued from Yankee vandals by the wife of one of Lincoln's cabinet members, who had them placed in storage and returned to the family after the war.

*W*hile on picket duty during the West Virginia campaign a German volunteer in Confederate service chanced to hear his native tongue coming from the Union lines; venturing a call in German, he heard in reply, "From what part do you come, countryman?" He responded "Bavaria," which elicited a rifle ball in his direction, sectionalism by no means being an exclusively American problem.

*C*onfederate Lt. James E. Hanger, who lost a leg as a result of wounds incurred at Philippi (3 June 1861), in what is now West Virginia, an action sometimes called the first battle of the war, devised for himself an artificial limb so superior to existing devices that he founded a firm for their manufacture which still exists.

At the battle of Wilson's Creek (10 August 1861), Confederate Brig. Gen. Sterling Price was grazed by a musket ball fired by one of Union Brig. Gen. Nathaniel Lyon's men, whereupon the corpulent Rebel remarked, "That isn't fair; if I were as slim as Lyon that fellow would have missed me entirely."

★ ★ ★

On 6 March 1861, over a month before the bombardment of Fort Sumter, at a time when the United States Army totalled but 16,000 men, Jefferson Davis, president of the Confederacy, issued a call for 100,000 volunteers to serve for one year.

★ ★ ★

Artillery pieces were in such short supply in the Confederacy in 1861 that some batteries received British 3-pounders, 6-pounders, and 8-inch howitzers captured in the War of 1812.

★ ★ ★

It is said that after a particularly wearing march shortly before the first battle of Bull Run his men were so exhausted that Thomas J. Jackson posted only one sentry for his brigade, the "Gallant Jackson" himself.

★ ★ ★

Aside from the fact that it had some uncertainty about its name, the principal distinction of the *59th New York—The Union Guard* or *The Van Guard* or *The United States Van Guard*—is that it was raised on the site where the author of this volume went to college, 302 Broadway in lower Manhattan, which was later for a time the headquarters of the Thompson submachinegun company.

★ ★ ★

The Union officers holding Ft. Sumter were supplied with cigars and claret through the courtesy of Confederate Brig. Gen. Pierre G.T. Beauregard, who was in command of the investing forces.

★ ★ ★

In August of 1861 the *79th New York Highlanders* mutinied when the army decided to take away their kilts, but were quickly brought to their senses when higher authorities presented an irrefutable argument in the form of a Regular Army battery.

★ ★ ★

*L*t. Manning M. Kimmel of the U.S. *2nd Cavalry* did not "go South" until shortly after serving at the first battle of Bull Run, and, after a career as a staff officer in the Confederate Army, went on to father Husband Kimmel, associated with another national military disaster on 7 December 1941.

Confederate gunners bombarding Ft. Sumter are reported to have cheered each time the defenders got off a shot in reply.

The sword which the secessionist ladies of Little Rock, Arkansas, awarded Capt. James Totten in February of 1861 for his decision not to defend the U.S. arsenal there when seized by the state, proved immensely useful over the next four years as he rose to become a Union brevet brigadier general.

The first battle of Bull Run is the only occasion in history on which the United States Marine Corps left the field in precipitous haste.

At the outbreak of the Civil War the Confederacy had 3,549 miles of coastline, with 189 ports, harbors and other navigable inlets.

Confederate Army regulations specified that uniform trousers were to be "sky blue," but, though well-heeled officers and regiments occasionally sported such in the early part of the war, there is no record of them ever being issued to the troops.

The first shot of the Civil War was either that signalling the start of the Confederate bombardment of Ft. Sumter discharged from a 10 inch mortar at 4:30 a.m. on 12 April 1861 by Lt. Wade Hampton Gibbes, of Capt. George S. James' battery, at Ft. Johnson, or, more accurately, those fired weeks earlier, on 9 January, when Ft. Moultrie warned off the Federal supply ship *Queen of the West* with a couple of rounds: whichever is preferred, the distinction of firing the momentous round certainly does not belong, as tradition has it, to secessionist fanatic Edmund Ruffin, who may, however, have fired the first round from the batteries on Cummings Point.

When the *55th Illinois* mustered into Federal service in 1861 there were 91 pairs of brothers among its 1,056 men: in four years of service, 58 of the brothers died in battle, amounting to over a third of the regiment's combat deaths.

*O*f the 10 Union officers in Ft. Sumter, 6 became major generals, 3 others, including 1 who resigned after the surrender to "go South," were killed in action early in the war, and one became a colonel.

★ ★ ★

*E*lizabeth Cooper Vernon of Philadelphia was so proficient in the use of firearms and in the manual of arms that, at the start of the war, she was engaged to drill a company of young men who had volunteered for service.

★ ★ ★

*T*he first of the 124 generals to die in action during the war was Confederate Brig. Gen. Robert S. Garnett, who fell on 13 July 1861, near Corrick's Ford, on the Cheat River in what is now West Virginia.

★ ★ ★

*W*hen a private who had wandered into his quarters at Manassas apologized for appropriating his desk, pen and paper to write a letter, Pierre G.T. Beauregard is said to have replied, "Sit down and finish your letter, my friend. You are very welcome, and can always come in here when you wish to write."

★ ★ ★

The Bowie knives, with which many volunteers equipped themselves early in the war, were later found to be worthless in battle but enormously useful for "carving beef and pork."

★ ★ ★

Thomas J. Jackson, a profoundly religious man, is said to have once refused to use a particular batch of gunpowder because it had been procured on the Sabbath.

★ ★ ★

Although some 4,000 shells were fired at or by Ft. Sumter over a period of 34 hours, not a single man was killed nor even wounded in the exchange.

★ ★ ★

At a meeting for the families of the *1st Vermont* early in the war, one woman arose to say how proud she was that she could do something for her country by having two sons in the ranks, and regretted only that 20 years earlier she had not had the foresight to provide more.

★ ★ ★

The Civil War was rough on the streets of New York: Gustavus W. Smith and Mansfield Lovell, respectively, the Street Commissioner and the Deputy Street Commissioner, both resigned their posts to take up appointments as major generals in the Confederate Army.

*T*old by William Tecumseh Sherman that he had only requested a colonelcy upon rejoining the army, Irvin McDowell expressed surprise, saying, "What? You should have asked for a brigadier general's rank. You're just as fit for it as I am," to which Sherman replied, "I know it."

*W*hile attempting to create an army at Manassas in the first weeks of the war, Pierre G.T. Beauregard discovered that his requisitions for rope to use in wells were being denied at Richmond because all rope was needed for the navy, which at that point had a handful of vessels.

*B*etween Lincoln's call for volunteers in mid-April and the end of 1861 over 50 regiments were raised in New York City.

★ ★ ★

*W*hen, at a meeting in mid-August of 1861, Lincoln heard William T. Sherman state that he had a strong desire to serve in a subordinate capacity, the president expressed immediate agreement with the request, noting that, "My chief trouble is to find places for the many generals who want to be at the head of affairs, to command armies, and so forth."

★ ★ ★

*T*he Confederacy's *1st Louisiana* probably holds the record for the most cosmopolitan outfit in the war, with 37 different nationalities represented in its ranks, although several New York regiments probably came close to matching this record.

★　★　★

*T*he senior Jewish officer in the Civil War was Commodore Uriah P. Levy (1792-1862), the owner of Jefferson's Monticello—which the Confederacy confiscated as "enemy property"—who retired in 1861, after 49 years of acrimony—he survived numerous duels, 6 courts-martial, and 2 cashierings—but generally distinguished service in the navy.

★　★　★

*J*oining the Confederate 6th Arkansas in 1861, Henry M. "Dr. Livingston, I presume" Stanley later fought at Shiloh and, being captured, immediately volunteered for duty with the Union, serving for a while with the army and later joining the navy.

★　★　★

*T*he first drill manual issued by North Carolina upon its secession was printed at The Institute for the Deaf and Dumb, and the Blind.

★　★　★

*R*ejecting Lincoln's first call for troops in April of 1861, Gov. Henry M. Rector of Arkansas said, "The people of this Commonwealth are free-men, not slaves," and began to press for immediate secession, conveniently overlooking the fact that over 25 percent of the people of Arkansas *were* slaves.

*F*rancis Scott "The Star-Spangled Banner" Key's entire family supported secession.

*T*he first Union victory at sea occurred in June of 1861, when William Tillman, the young black cook of the schooner *S.J. Waring,* single-handedly recaptured the ship from a crew off the Confederate privateer *Jeff Davis,* killing three and capturing three, which feat he is said to have accomplished in little more than seven minutes. Congress awarded him $6,000 in prize money.

*N*early one-third of the 2,952 Union men killed or injured at First Bull Run were from New York City.

The first battlefield monument commemorating a Civil War hero was that to Confederate Col. Francis Bartow of the *8th Georgia*, erected in September of 1861 on the spot where he had fallen while commanding a brigade on the previous 21 July, during the battle of Bull Run.

★　★　★

The only Regular Army officer born in the Deep South to remain loyal to his oath was Capt. Benjamin Franklin Davis, a Mississippian, who went on to command the *1st California Cavalry* and later the *8th New York Cavalry* with considerable ability until killed in action at Brandy Station on 9 June 1863.

★　★　★

Samuel Cooper, the senior general in the Confederate Army, was born in Dutchess County, New York.

★　★　★

At the outbreak of the war the Rev. B.C. Ward, pastor of a Congregational church in Genesco, Illinois, attempted to raise an infantry company composed entirely of clergymen.

*L*ate in 1861 the Hungarian General George Klapka—a very fine commander—offered his services to the Union, expressing a willingness to accept the post of general-in-chief in return for a cash advance of $100,000 plus an annual salary of $25,000, though stipulating that he would serve as chief-of-the-general-staff until he learned English.

★ ★ ★

*W*hen a pompous young lieutenant answered his challenge by calling out "Ass!" a sentry is said to have responded, "Advance, ass, and give the countersign."

★ ★ ★

*F*our regiments raised in Philadelphia in the spring of 1861 were for a time known as the *1st, 2nd, 3rd* and *5th California,* since Sen. James A. McDougall of the "Golden State" helped foot the bill for their recruiting: later redesignated the *71st, 72nd, 69th*—an Irish outfit which wanted the same number as New York's famed Irish regiment—and *106th Pennsylvania,* the regiments went on to distinguish themselves as the *Philadelphia Brigade,* among other things holding The Angle at Gettysburg.

★ ★ ★

The first Confederate warship to show the flag in a European port was the lightly armed side-wheeler C.S.S. *Nashville,* which landed at Southampton on 21 November 1861.

During the battle of Corrick's Ford in West Virginia (13 July 1861), an Indiana Methodist preacher not only battled mightily for the Lord, but also for the Union, appending to each shot the line "And may the Lord have mercy on your soul!"

When organized in October of 1861, the *6th Pennsylvania Cavalry* was equipped as lancers, toting 9-foot pig-stickers and pistols into action, rather than sabers and carbines; despite the near-total inutility of the regiment's armament, "Rush's Lancers" were not re-equipped as a proper cavalry regiment until June of 1863, possibly because they looked good on parade.

During the first battle of Bull Run there were present in the vicinity of the field at least one governor, six senators and ten representatives, in addition to one president, Yankees all save the last, who was Jefferson Davis.

*W*hen Hetty Cary—one of a trio of cousins who were the "prettiest women in Virginia" and outstanding lights of Richmond social life during the war—waved a Confederate flag from her Baltimore window as a Federal regiment marched by, the colonel declined to arrest her because, "She is beautiful enough to do as she damned pleases."

*T*here is a tale that when a Felix von Salm-Salm informed Lincoln that he was a scion of one of the oldest and noblest families in Germany, the president replied, "Oh, never mind that, you will not find that to be an obstacle to your advancement."

*O*f 500 men raised in San Francisco who were enrolled as the *California Battalion of the 2nd Massachusetts,* fully 10 percent eventually became officers.

*T*he attack in Baltimore by a secessionist mob on the men of the *6th Massachusetts* on 19 April 1861 occurred on the 86th anniversary of the day that Bay Staters' grandfathers fired "The shot heard 'round the world."

*A*lthough flogging was abolished by the Union Army in August of 1861 and by the Confederates the following April, the practice was not entirely eliminated until after the war.

★ ★ ★

*A*s the *3rd Maine* was preparing to depart for the war, the patriotic ladies of Augusta distributed over 50 bushels of doughnuts to their brave boys in blue, roughly 10,000 sinkers in all their infinite variety, including square, long, triangular and round ones, twisted, untwisted and double twisted ones, holed and unholed ones, light risen and hard kneaded ones, with numerous flavors, coatings and fillings.

★ ★ ★

*M*iss Sally L. Tompkins of Richmond was made a captain of cavalry—becoming the only woman ever to hold a commission in the Confederate Army—by Jefferson Davis on 9 September 1861 because a hospital which she had established after First Bull Run proved to have a remarkable recovery rate.

★ ★ ★

*T*he *5th Pennsylvania Cavalry Regiment* appears to have the distinction of being the largest unit in the history of the United States Army to be composed primarily of Jewish personnel.

*R*ichard A. Pryor, a Virginian on the staff of Pierre G.T. Beauregard, was very nearly the first man to die in the Civil War when, paying a call on Fort Sumter to help arrange its surrender, he took a draught of what he thought was brandy, only to discover that it was iodine, but was saved from this dubious honor by Union Surgeon Samuel W. Crawford—later a major general—who administered a stomach pumping.

★ ★ ★

*D*uring the first year of the war there were nearly 4,000 cases of illness for every 1,000 men in the Union armies.

★ ★ ★

On the eve of the war the United States Navy had 1,457 officers, warrant officers and midshipmen on duty, of whom 259 line officers and 73 other officers resigned, for a total of 332, or 22.7 percent of the naval officer corps. The Marine Corps, which had 63 officers, lost 22 (34.9 percent) to the Confederacy, one of whom became a general. Of some 200 officers in the Revenue Marine—the precursor of the Coast Guard—and the Coast Survey, about 60 (30.0 percent) resigned, several of whom turned their ships over to the Confederacy, an act which no resigning naval officer emulated. Thus, of about 1,720 officers in the seagoing services, about 404 (23.4 percent) resigned, a figure significantly lower than that for army officers. Unfortunately it is not possible to analyze the regional origins of these officers.

On the eve of the Civil War there were approximately 15,000 enlisted men in the army, 7,600 in the navy plus 1,000 in the Marine Corps, and perhaps 1,200 more in the Revenue Marine and Coast Survey. While the regional origins of these men cannot be determined, it is reasonable to assume that a significant proportion of them were from the South, yet only 26 army enlisted men are known to have gone South, in contrast to the 313 officers.

$\star$ $\star$ $\star$

At the outbreak of the Civil War Samuel F.B. Morse, artist and inventor of the "Morse Code," suggested that "Old Glory" be divided in half diagonally, from the upper hoist to the lower fly, with the upper half to be used by the North and the lower by the South, each side replacing the missing portion with a white field, thus symbolizing the sundering of the old nation and expressing hope for its eventual reunification. This and other proposals to remove the "seceded" stars from the "Stars and Stripes," were all quashed by Lincoln, who pointed out that the states had never left the Union.

At least one woman served as a "drummer boy" during the Civil War, a resident of Brooklyn named Emily, who disguised herself as a boy and enlisted in Michigan, serving in the *Army of the Cumberland* until mortally wounded at Lookout Mountain.

1862

---

*A*mong the many technical innovations on
the famed U.S.S. *Monitor,* is the often overlooked
fact that she was the first warship to have flush
toilets.

★ ★ ★

A badly chafed heel forced Confederate
Maj. Gen. James Longstreet to fight the battle of
Antietam wearing a pair of "clumsy carpet slippers."

★ ★ ★

*E*arly in the war the Union armies were
using 600 different types of artillery ammunition.

★ ★ ★

In order to warm himself one cold day in January of 1862 the usually abstemious Stonewall Jackson took a glass of whiskey in the mistaken belief that it was wine, with the result that he very soon opened his coat, complaining that it was too warm, and talked more freely than at any other time in the war.

★ ★ ★

As a result of Union Maj. Gen George McClellan's Peninsula campaign, the Confederate Army acquired some 60,000 Yankee overcoats.

★ ★ ★

During the hottest part of the battle of Fair Oaks (31 May to 1 June 1862), two men of the *2nd Connecticut* "got at loggerheads" with each other, threw down their muskets and fell to at fisticuffs— had it out, picked up their arms and pitched into the Rebels again."

★ ★ ★

Enlisted for occupation and security duty, the *37th Iowa* was composed entirely of men over 45 years of age: the average was 57, and a few men were well up in their 70s and one in his 80s.

★ ★ ★

*D*uring a truce after the battle of Munfordville in September of 1862, Union Col. John Thomas Wilder of the *17th Indiana* lent Confederate Brig. Gen. James R. Chalmers shovels so that he could dispose of his dead.

*B*ecause a newspaper story mentioned that he was smoking a cigar during the Confederate breakout attempt at Fort Donelson, patriotic citizens in the North sent Ulysses S. Grant over 10,000 stogies in all their infinite variety.

*T*he 12,000 Union troops taken prisoner by Stonewall Jackson at Harper's Ferry on 15 September 1862 was the largest surrender of troops in the history of the United States Army until the Japanese took 40,000 men on Bataan on 9 April 1942.

*A*s night began to fall at the battle of Perryville on 8 October 1862, a Union officer who was bringing his troops into action, spotted a general and said, "I have come to your assistance with my brigade, sir," and went to identify his outfit, whereupon Confederate Lt. Gen. Leonidas Polk replied, "There is some mistake about this. You are my prisoner."

*O*ne day, finding that the entire Cabinet was opposed to a proposal which he had made, Lincoln smiled and said, "The measure passes by a majority of one."

★ ★ ★

*B*etween those working the streets and those in the approximately 450 "sporting houses," there were an estimated 7,500 "ladies of the evening" in Washington in early 1862.

★ ★ ★

*E*spying an ill-dressed soldier swaying badly on the back of a horse, a thirsty Confederate straggler asked, "Where did you get your liquor from? Give me some!" only to discover that the man in question was Thomas "Stonewall" Jackson, who, although the most careless dresser and the worst horseman in the Confederate Army, was also the most abstemious.

★ ★ ★

*T*he first national conscription law in American history was passed by the Confederate Congress on 16 April 1862.

*W*ithin a year of the start of the war, Confederate Gen. Pierre G.T. Beauregard's black hair had turned almost completely gray, a development which his friends attributed to the pressures of war but less charitable—and more accurate—folks suggested it was because the Federal blockade had cut off the supply of dye.

*O*n 17 September 1862 Yankee Col. John T. Wilder, an amateur soldier, commanding Union forces besieged in Munfordville, Kentucky, was uncertain as to protocol in such situations and so asked Confederate Maj. Gen. Simon Bolivar Buckner for advice, which the latter honorably refused to give, though he did permit Wilder to inspect the investing forces, whereupon Wilder said "I believe I'll surrender," and did.

*T*he battle flag of a Confederate infantry regiment measured 48" by 48," while that of a Union regiment was 72" by 78."

*T*he *131st* and *133rd New York,* which mustered into Federal service in July of 1862, were recruited largely through the efforts of the New York City police, who later also helped raise the *161st, 173rd* and *174th New York Infantry* and the *14th New York Cavalry.*

*A*t the battle of Shiloh all six of the division commanders in the Union Army of the Tennessee were lawyers: Stephen A. Hurlbut, John A. McClernand, Benjamin M. Prentiss, William Tecumseh Sherman, Lew Wallace and W.H.L Wallace.

★ ★ ★

*W*hile there was considerable international tension over the "Trent Affair," when a Union warship removed Confederate officials from a British merchant ship, the crisis was resolved so courteously that in February of 1862 several thousand British troops were permitted to cross Maine on route to Canada, where they had been sent to beef up the garrison in the event of war with the United States.

★ ★ ★

*W*hen none of his staff could tell George B. McClellan how deep the Chickahominy River was, Lt. George A. Custer put spurs to horse, plunged in, rode across, turned around, rode back and, as his mount regained the bank, said "That's how deep it is, General."

★ ★ ★

*T*hough the *53rd New York* ["The d'Epineuil Zouaves"] was recruited by Col. Jobert d'Epineuil in August of 1861 for three years service, it proved so full of goldbrickers, drunks, brawlers and rowdies that it was discharged the following March.

*C*onfederate Brig. Gen. Nathan "Shanks" Evans, a fine tactical commander, had an orderly who carried his "barrelita," a special wooden container which held a gallon of whiskey, just in case the general had the need for a drop in the midst of battle.

*I*n the darkness which engulfed the field at Perryville on the night of 8 October 1862, Confederate Lt. Gen. Leonidas Polk rode up to a colonel and angrily admonished him for firing into friendly troops, only to discover that he had blundered into the Yankee lines, whereupon he ordered the regiment to cease fire and rode slowly down the line until he could make his escape.

*W*hen Union forces took Memphis on 6 June 1862, they pressed into service several captured Confederate rams and gunboats, the smallest of which was named *General Pillow* in joking reference to one of the most inept and least courageous of Confederate generals.

*C*onfederate Maj. Gen. Edward "Allegheny" Johnson was often called "Old Clubby" because he was wont to lead his troops into battle waving a heavy old walking stick rather than the more traditional sword.

★ ★ ★

*D*uring 1862 the *Army of the Potomac* had an average of 28 wagons for every 1,000 men.

★ ★ ★

*A*mong the many prisoners taken when Confederate Brig. Gen. Nathan Bedford Forrest's troopers captured Holly Springs, Mississippi, on 20 December 1862, was Julia Grant, the wife of Union Maj. Gen. Ulysses S. Grant, who was shortly passed through the lines.

★ ★ ★

*P*ursuing a wounded Confederate officer at Shiloh on 7 April 1862, Col. A.K. Johnson of the *28th Illinois* attempted to grab the man by his hair only to have it come away in his hand leaving him holding a wig.

★ ★ ★

*T*he situation at the surrender of Ft. Donelson on 16 February 1862 was so confused that Confederate Brig. Gen. Bushrod R. Johnson was able to escape merely by walking calmly through the Yankee lines.

★ ★ ★

*W*hen the *3rd* *Wisconsin* broke at the battle of Winchester (25 May 1862), Maj. Gen. Nathaniel Banks called out, "Stop men! Don't you love your country?" whereupon one of the fleeing men replied, "Yes, by God, and I'm going back to it just as fast as I can."

*W*hen the Orleans Guards, a Louisiana volunteer battalion, went into action at Shiloh, they discovered that their stylish blue uniforms had the unfortunate effect of causing their Rebel comrades to mistake them for Yankees, so they reversed their coats and fought all day with the white linings showing.

*O*f 583 Union generals, 188 (32.3 percent) had no military experience prior to the Civil War, as did 153 (36 percent) of 425 Confederate generals.

*T*he yacht *America*, which captured the "Queen's Cup" in 1851 and began the famed series of races which still bear her name, served as a blockade runner during the Civil War and was sunk off Charleston in early 1862.

*O*ne of the most important battles of 1862 was fought on 5 May, when 1,500 Mexican troops armed with Brown Bess muskets and Baker rifles—British war-surplus which had been used at Waterloo in 1815—soundly thrashed 7,500 Frenchmen at Puebla, thereby keeping Mexico City in *Juarista* hands for another year.

★ ★ ★

*D*uring one of the many campaigns in '62, a weary Robert E. Lee took a nap by the side of a road, down which shortly came a division of his doughtiest warriors, who, seeing their beloved commander at rest, hushed their voices and lightened their tread lest they disturb him.

★ ★ ★

*I*t required the personal intervention of Abraham Lincoln to get Congress to authorize the enlistment of chaplains of the Jewish faith.

★ ★ ★

*N*ot inclined to give the benefit of the doubt to a foreigner, Confederate troops referred to Prince Camille Armand Jules Marie de Polignac as "Polecat" until their first battle with him, when he led them into the fray crying, "Now you will see whether I am a 'Polecat' or a 'Polignac,' Charge!"

★ ★ ★

*B*y mid-1862 Union Army bakeries at Fortress Monroe in Virginia were turning out 30,000 loaves of bread a day.

★　★　★

*T*he Confederate defenses at Ft. Henry on the Tennessee River were so badly designed that, when some Federal naval officers rowed over to accept the surrender of the place on 6 February 1862, their boat floated right through the sally port, the Tennessee River being then in flood.

★　★　★

*T*he turret of U.S.S *Monitor* was made by the Novelty Iron Works.

★　★　★

*O*ne of Union Maj. Gen. Daniel Butterfield's most important services to the war effort—and to American military tradition—occurred one beautifully calm night during the Peninsula campaign, when, as the *Army of the Potomac* lay encamped at Harrison's Landing, he composed "Taps."

★　★　★

*D*uring the attack on the Confederate forts guarding Hatteras Inlet on 28 August 1862, a Union warship, believing it was bombarding enemy cavalry, decimated a herd of beef cattle.

*T*he mascot of the *6th Iowa* was a mongrel named "Jeff Davis."

★ ★ ★

*A*lthough the famous clash between U.S.S. *Monitor* and C.S.S. *Virginia* on 9 March 1862 ushered in the age of ironclad warships, neither vessel suffered a single man killed or permanently injured.

★ ★ ★

*T*he troops could always tell when Confederate Maj. Gen. Sterling Price was getting ready to fight, because he invariably wore a certain multicolored plaid hunting shirt which they nicknamed his "war coat."

★ ★ ★

*W*hen, at Corinth, Mississippi, on 30 May 1862, a Union officer refused to permit some Sanitary Commission workers to provide his brigade with fresh water, an imperious female voice was heard to cry "Halt!" which the troops immediately did, much to the chagrin of their commander, who knew the fate of those who crossed "Mother" Bickerdyke.

★ ★ ★

One chilly day late in 1862, a group of Yankees chanced to come upon some Rebels engaged in baptizing a comrade in the Rapidan River, whereupon they joined in the hymn singing.

Maj. Gen. Edwin Vose Sumner, the oldest corps commander in the *Army of the Potomac,* was nicknamed "Bull Head" because a musket ball supposedly bounced off his head.

Among the many activities in which they indulged when they had nothing better to do while in camp, the troops of both armies were wont to pass the time by staging lice races.

Curtis King, who was 80 when he joined the *37th Iowa* in November of 1862, was probably the oldest enlisted man in the war, and was further distinguished by having several sons, 20 grandsons and four or five great-grandsons all in blue.

One unusual aspect of the Confederate attack on Corinth, Mississippi on 3 October 1862 was the fact that there was an earthquake as the troops were moving into position.

*W*hen Union troops captured Fort Pulaski, Georgia on 11 April 1862, the newly appointed commander, Col. Alfred H. Terry of the *7th Connecticut*, summoned his Confederate predecessor, a Colonel Olmstead, and lent him $50 to tide him over any inconvenience which might occur while he was a prisoner-of-war.

★ ★ ★

*I*n order to provide a landing force to support the Union river flotilla on the Mississippi, the *Mississippi Marine Brigade* was formed from army volunteers in mid-1862, comprising the *1st Battalion Mississippi Marine Brigade Infantry,* the *Mississippi Marine Brigade Light Artillery Battery* and, inevitably, the *1st Battalion Mississippi Marine Brigade Cavalry;* appropriately enough, the "horse marines" were raised in Missouri.

★ ★ ★

*G*eorge B. McClellan's movement of the bulk of the *Army of the Potomac* by water from Washington to the Virginia Peninsula in late March of 1862 was the largest seaborne movement of troops in history until World War I.

★ ★ ★

*W*hen questioned by some Indiana troops as to whether she was "Secesh" or "Union," an old mountain woman replied, "A Baptist, an' always have been."

★ ★ ★

Coming upon an abandoned gun during the battle of Antietam, Confederate Maj. Gen. James Longstreet and his staff proceeded to put it into action, serving the piece until a less exalted crew could be gotten together.

★　★　★

In July of 1862 the War Department discovered that the Union armies had 1 musician for every 41 soldiers, a ratio which was soon sharply reduced when regimental bands were abolished.

★　★　★

Edward C. Stockton had perhaps the most unusual military career of anyone in the Civil War: graduating from Annapolis in 1850, he was shortly after expelled from the Navy and engaged in various civilian pursuits until the war broke out, whereupon he became successively a lieutenant in the South Carolina State Navy in early 1861, a second lieutenant in the Confederate States Marine Corps from May through September of that year, then a captain in the 21st South Carolina from January through April of 1862 and thereafter an officer in the Confederate States Navy, rising to lieutenant.

★　★　★

At Shiloh the *2nd Texas* fought in undyed uniforms which greatly resembled shrouds, eliciting remarks such as, "Who were them hellcats who went into battle dressed in their grave-clothes?"

★　★　★

Maj. Gen. William Wilkens of the Pennsylvania militia was undoubtedly the oldest officer in the war, being 83 when commissioned in 1862.

★　★　★

When after the battle of Chantilly (1 September 1862), the body of a Union general was brought to him, Stonewall Jackson took one look at the dead man's face, and, lifting his hat, said, "My God, boys, you know who you have killed? You have shot the most gallant officer in the United States Army. This is Phil Kearny, who lost his arm in the Mexican War."

★　★　★

Over 75 percent of the 15,000 Union graves in the Fredericksburg National Cemetery are marked "unknown."

*W*hen, in late 1862 the Union commander at New Orleans, Maj. Gen. Benjamin F. Butler—nicknamed "Beast" by Southerners for his lack of noble qualities—learned that Caroline Beauregard was seriously ill, he offered her husband, Confederate Gen. Pierre G.T. Beauregard, a pass through Federal lines so that he might visit her, an offer which the latter declined: when Mrs. Beauregard died early the following year, the Union provided a steamboat to carry her remains to her native parish.

★   ★   ★

*T*he youngest officer in the war was undoubtedly E.G. Baxter (born 10 September 1849), who enlisted in the Confederate 7th Kentucky in June of 1862 and was made a second lieutenant when not quite 14.

★   ★   ★

*W*hen an officer commented that a certain major known in the army as a shirker had been wounded and would be unable to perform a particular assignment, Stonewall Jackson is said to have commented "Wounded! If it really is so, I think it must have been by an accidental discharge of his duty."

★   ★   ★

*T*he fright which a young Confederate soldier experienced when Maj. Gen. Benjamin F. Cheatham discovered him up a tree stealing fruit quickly turned to relief when the latter said, "Young man, drop me down a few of those fine apples."

★ ★ ★

*T*he first income tax in American history was instituted by the Union on 1 July 1862, a measure which was copied in the Confederacy nine months later.

★ ★ ★

*A*las for romance, it is not true that the last silk dresses in the Confederacy were captured by the Federals on 4 June 1862, during the Peninsula campaign, in the form of a stray balloon which had been made through the generosity of the ladies of Richmond.

★ ★ ★

*W*hen asked why he never touched alcoholic beverages, Stonewall Jackson remarked, "Why, sir, because I like the taste of them, and when I discovered that to be the case I made up my mind at once to do without them altogether."

*S*o radical was John Ericsson's proposed warship *Monitor,* that his contract with the Navy included a clause requiring repayment of all monies advanced if she were unable to steam at 8 knots for 12 miles.

★ ★ ★

*W*hen asked by the secretary of war if he had organized a regiment of "fugitive slaves," Union Brig. Gen. David Hunter, serving on the Carolina coast, replied that he had not, but that he did have "a fine regiment of persons whose late masters are 'fugitive rebels'."

★ ★ ★

*T*hroughout all of his campaigns Thomas "Stonewall" Jackson was wont to suck on lemons, though no one could ever figure out how he obtained them.

★ ★ ★

*A*s a result of a "personal encounter" with Union Brig. Gen. Jefferson C. Davis on 29 September 1862, Union Maj. Gen. William Nelson died of a bullet in the chest, for which Davis was never brought to account.

*W*hen some of his troops seemed hesitant under fire at the battle of Winchester (Sunday, 25 May 1862), Confederate Brig. Gen. Richard Taylor shouted, "What the hell are you dodging for?" whereupon Stonewall Jackson, who "never condoned cursing, especially on the Sabbath" turned to him and in a mild voice said, "I am afraid you are a wicked fellow."

★ ★ ★

*W*hen a Yankee Kentuckian chanced to be captured by his Rebel brother during the battle of Shiloh, he admonished the latter to take care not to fire at a particular Union officer since "that's father."

★ ★ ★

*S*ince the troops usually preferred something with a little alcohol in it, they often resorted to various time-honored soldier's concoctions, such as "champagne," a fermented beverage made with three parts of water and one of corn and molasses.

★ ★ ★

*O*ne winter's night near Fredericksburg, a Federal band struck up a number of patriotic tunes, and, when one of the Rebels listening from across the Rappahannock shouted, "Now give us some of ours," ran through some Southern airs as well, ending the program with "Home, Sweet Home," amid cheers from both armies.

*A*t the battle of Pea Ridge (7–8 March 1862) some Confederate Indian troops, having captured a Union cannon, put its carriage to the torch, with consequent casualties when the loaded piece blew up spectacularly.

*W*hen a pro-Confederate Englishwoman visiting his studio in Florence, Italy, asked American sculptor Thomas Powers if he had ever executed a bust of Jefferson Davis, he replied, "No madam, but I hope that before long, an artist of another profession than mine will have the pleasure of executing him."

*S*o infrequently did Thomas "Stonewall" Jackson draw his sword that it eventually rusted in the scabbard.

"*O*ld Abe," the eagle mascot of the *8th Wisconsin*, served four years in the field, participating in 42 battles, during which he was once wounded, before being put to honorable retirement in special quarters at the Wisconsin state capital, where he perished in a fire in 1881.

*D*uring the Second Bull Run campaign (August–September 1862), Confederate cavalryman J.E.B. Stuart chanced to "capture" Union Maj. Gen. John Pope's dress coat, while the former's best plumed hat fell into the hands of the latter, with the result that Stuart proposed a formal exchange of prisoners.

★ ★ ★

*O*ne of the first black regiments mustered into Federal service was the *1st Louisiana Native Guards,* originally organized—but rejected—for Confederate service by the free blacks of the state at the onset of the war.

★ ★ ★

*W*hen, during the battle of Murfreesboro, Confederate Maj. Gen. Benjamin Cheatham shouted "Forward, boys, and give 'em hell, boys," his superior, Lt. Gen. Leonidas Polk, agreeing in principal, but, as an Episcopal bishop, unwilling to utter profanity, shouted "Give 'em what General Cheatham says, boys! Give 'em what General Cheatham says!"

*L*ee's three sons all saw service in the Confederate Army: George Washington Lee and William Henry Fitzhugh Lee rising to major generals,
while his youngest, Robert E. Lee, Jr., enlisted as a
private and rose to a captaincy in the artillery. The
senior Lee's brother, Sydney Smith Lee, became a
captain in the Confederate Navy, while his nephew,
Fitzhugh Lee, became a lieutenant general in the
Confederacy. Several cousins served the Union,
notably Samuel P. Lee and Roger Jones, who were
naval officers, and William R. Terrill, who fell as a
brigadier general, as did his brother, James, though
he fought for the South.

★ ★ ★

*A*bout 75 black men—some estimates place
the figure as high as 100—held commissions as
officers, mostly in company grades in the Louisiana
regiments. Nine black men attained the rank of
major and one became a brevet lieutenant colonel,
Dr. Alexander T. Augusta, a Canadian physician
who gave up a lucrative practice in Toronto to fight
for the Union. In addition, Lt. Col. William N.
Reed of the *1st North Carolina Volunteers* (*35th U.S.
Colored Infantry*) was widely considered to have been
"bound to both races by the ties of consanguinity."

★ ★ ★

On 13 October 1862 the Confederate Congress authorized the award of a decoration to men "conspicuous for courage and good conduct on the field of battle." Such men were to be elected by the troops of their company after each engagement in which the company had been particularly distinguished. No awards were ever made under this provision. However, another measure provided for the publication of a "Roll of Honor" after each engagement, which was to be read to the troops at a formal parade, a practice which continued almost to the end of the war. In addition, about 200 men in both the army and navy received special promotions for "Valor and Skill" under the terms of an act adopted in April of 1862, and a number of officers were voted the "Thanks of Congress."

★ ★ ★

Compared to the numbers of men in the armies, the manpower of the sea services—navy, marines, revenue service—was relatively insignificant. Officially there were 132,544 enlistments in Union forces afloat, although the Navy peaked at some 50,100 men at the end of the war, including about 3,500 Marines, while total enlistments in the Confederate sea services were probably between 12,000 and 15,000 men, although the peak strength of the Confederate Navy appears to have been about 5,000, plus about 1,000 Marines—figures attained in early 1864.

1863

On 1 January 1863, the eve of the final day at Murfreesboro, Union and Confederate bands alternated with each other for several hours playing war songs until someone struck up "Home, Sweet Home," which was immediately taken up by bands in both armies and by most of the men as well.

★ ★ ★

Arthur MacArthur, who in 1899 rather belatedly received a Medal of Honor for leading his regiment at Missionary Ridge in 1863, was the father of Douglas MacArthur, who received his during World War II, making them the only father and son to have ever received this decoration.

★ ★ ★

By mid-1863 it was estimated that the war was costing the Federal government $2,500,000 a day.

★ ★ ★

Catching a young soldier stealing a ham from his wagon, Union Maj. Gen. William T. Sherman discovered that as a result of a commissary mix-up the boy's regiment hadn't been issued rations in several days and said, "Take the ham then, and whenever you need any more come to me and ask for them."

★ ★ ★

The officers of the Russian fleet which wintered in New York in 1863–1864 donated $4,760 to buy fuel for the poor of the city.

★ ★ ★

When a Southern belle tearfully implored Union Maj. Gen. William S. Rosecrans for permission to pass through the Federal lines to visit an ailing uncle, the general replied, "Very sorry indeed, madam. My uncle has been indisposed for some time. As soon as Uncle Sam recovers a little, you shall have a pass to go where you please."

★ ★ ★

During the three days of the battle of Gettysburg an estimated 566 tons of ammunition were expended, amounting to about 24 pounds for every casualty on both sides.

★ ★ ★

*I*t was said that on Stonewall Jackson's death some angels came down to escort him into heaven, only to find that he had beaten them to it by making a rapid flank march.

*N*ot only was Union Col. Benjamin Grierson, who commanded one of the most successful cavalry raids of the war, a music teacher wont to play the jew's-harp while leading his troops, but he disliked horses.

*C*onfederate Brig. Gen. Lewis A. Armistead had trouble keeping his hat on the point of his sword as he led the vanguard during Pickett's Charge at Gettysburg, for the weapon was so sharp it kept cutting the cloth, so that the hat kept slipping down the blade and he several times had to reposition it at the tip.

*A*s the battle of Chickamauga opened, a Confederate chaplain exhorted some troops to do their best for the cause, concluding, "Remember, boys, that he who is killed will sup tonight in paradise," whereupon one of the troops called back, "Come along and take supper with us."

*E*dmund Kirby, West Point '61, had the most meteoric promotion in the Union Army, being jumped from first lieutenant to brigadier general by direct order of Abraham Lincoln as he lay dying from a mortal wound incurred while commanding a battery at Chancellorsville with "undaunted courage."

★ ★ ★

*A*t one point during the retreat from Gettysburg Robert E. Lee's pet hen—she would lay an egg under his camp bed each morning—got lost, which upset him so much that he ordered a search and was not satisfied until she was found.

★ ★ ★

*T*he *10th New York Infantry* had its own Masonic lodge, the National Zouave Lodge, and often held regular meetings, even when in the field, to which fellow-Masons of the Confederate persuasion were welcome, if they happened to be around as prisoners-of-war.

★ ★ ★

*W*hen, during the battle of Gettysburg, Union Brig. Gen. Samuel Crawford reached down from his mount to grab the colors of the *1st Pennsylvania Reserves* in order to lead it in an attack, color bearer Cpl. Bertless Slott, unwilling to abandon his duty, grabbed the leg of the general's trousers and hung on, racing beside him as he charged the enemy.

★ ★ ★

On meeting Harriet Beecher Stowe, author of *Uncle Tom's Cabin,* Lincoln is said to have remarked, "So this is the little woman who wrote the book that made this big war."

★ ★ ★

During the Gettysburg campaign one of Hood's Texas Brigade noted that a patriotic woman of Chambersburg, Pennsylvania, had pinned the national colors to her ample bosom, and remarked, "Take care, madam, for Hood's boys are great at storming breastworks when the Yankee colors is on them," which prompted her to "beat a precipitate retreat."

★ ★ ★

Knowing of the suffering which the blockade was causing among the staunchly anti-slavery cotton mill workers in England, the American International Relief Committee was set up in New York in the winter of 1863 and dispatched the ship *George Griswold* with a load of relief supplies, thereby earning the thanks of the working people of England, and not a little political benefit besides.

★ ★ ★

Counting those enrolled on both sides, at least 3,200 women served as paid army nurses during the war.

Instructions for the Government of the Armies of the United States in the Field, prepared by Prof. Francis Lieber of Columbia University and issued by the War Department as "General Orders Number 100" in mid-1863, were the first formally stated rules of engagement ever issued by any power.

★ ★ ★

*W*hen Robert E. Lee rode by as the Confederate Army marched by on the road to Gettysburg, a patriotic Chambersburg matron ceased waving the "Stars and Stripes" long enough to cry, "O, I wish he was ours!"

★ ★ ★

*A*s the Confederate troops were falling back from Pickett's Charge at Gettysburg, British military observer Lt. Col. James Fremantle said, "I wouldn't have missed this for anything," to which Lt. Gen. James Longstreet replied, "The devil you wouldn't! I would like to have missed it very much. . . !"

★ ★ ★

*D*uring the Civil War the Confederacy issued about 200 different types of bonds and 582 types of paper currency.

★ ★ ★

Union cavalryman Elon Farnsworth's promotion to brigadier general came so unexpectedly that he had to borrow a suitable uniform from Maj. Gen. Alfred Pleasonton, which he was wearing when killed at Gettysburg four days later on 3 July 1863.

When a gentleman walked into a bookstore in Richmond to inquire about Victor Hugo's new novel *Les Miserables,* his inept effort to pronounce the title caused the salesclerk to remark, "Well, Lee's miserables are good enough to lick the Yankees!"

At the gate to the cemetery in Gettysburg, where some of the heaviest fighting took place on the first day of the battle, there was a sign which read, "All persons found using firearms in these grounds will be prosecuted with the utmost rigor of the law."

When asked by Braxton Bragg, "Do you know what a retreat looks like?," one of his men replied, "I ought to know, General, I've been with you during the entire campaign."

*W*hen an officer protested to Col. A. Van Horne Ellis of the *124th New York* that by mounting in the face of a Confederate attack on the second day at Gettysburg, he and Maj. James Cromwell were exposing themselves unnecessarily, the colonel replied, "The men must see us this day," and did so anyway, falling in action shortly afterwards.

★ ★ ★

*T*he first American actress to appear in the nude was Adah Isaacs Menken (1835-1868), who bared all for her art in a performance of Byron's *Mazeppa* on the New York stage in 1863.

★ ★ ★

*W*hile enduring the Confederate bombardment atop Cemetery Ridge on the third day of Gettysburg, Union Brig. Gen. John Gibbon may perhaps have received some satisfaction from the knowledge that the enemy was using his *The Artillerist's Manual* as their basic handbook.

★ ★ ★

*U*nion Rear Adm. David Dixon Porter was so fond of horses that he kept several aboard his Mississippi River Squadron flagship, U.S.S. *Black Hawk,* and was wont to gallop ashore over the gangplank for a ride now and again.

★ ★ ★

*T*he table of organization of the *Army of the Potomac* provided for artillery "brigades" because the chief of artillery, Henry J. Hunt, disliked the word "battalion."

★ ★ ★

*A*lthough the uniform regulations of both armies mandated its use throughout the war, it is unlikely that most of the troops ever even saw a cravat.

★ ★ ★

*W*hen Brig. Gen. Lewis A. Armistead—the point man of the "High Tide of the Confederacy"—on 3 July 1863 fell into Union hands, the mortally wounded officer recognized among his captors Sgt. Frederick Fuger with whom he had served in the Old Army, and who had manned the last Union piece in action as the Armistead's Rebels swept atop Cemetery Ridge to whom he said, "I thought it was you, sergeant. If I had known that you were in command of that battery I would never have led the charge against you."

★ ★ ★

*I*n the 19 days from their crossing of the Mississippi below Grand Gulf on 30 April 1863 to the investment of Vicksburg on 18 May, Maj. Gen. U. S. Grant's troops marched 180 miles, won 5 battles, captured 6,000 Confederate prisoners with nearly 100 pieces of artillery, and crossed countless small rivers and streams, all after having abandoned their line of supply.

*U*nion troops at Gettysburg captured 31 Confederate battle flags, the largest haul in the war not associated with a surrender.

*H*earing that someone had secured exemption from the draft because he had one leg shorter than the other, a Virginia country boy decided that he too could gain an exemption, and advanced the claim that he had "both legs too short."

*P*vt. Billy Crump of the *23rd Ohio,* orderly to Col. Rutherford B. Hayes, who later went on to greater things, was one of the most skilled foragers in the war, once returning from a 20-mile excursion with 50 chickens, 2 turkeys, a goose, some two dozen eggs, and nearly 30 pounds of butter.

★ ★ ★

*D*uring the Gettysburg campaign, Secretary of War Edwin M. Stanton reasoned that a good deal of money could be saved if the army did not supply uniforms to the many militiamen and volunteers who turned out to help stem Lee's invasion of Pennsylvania, since the emergency was certain to be over before their own clothing wore out. Lincoln demurred, however, and the men got their uniforms anyway.

*W*hen a Yankee sniper interrupted his service one Sunday morning, Confederate Chaplain Isaac T. Tichenor grabbed a musket, dispatched the man to his Maker, and went back to his prayers.

*I*n a counterattack on the second day at Gettysburg the *1st Minnesota* lost 82 percent of its 262 men, the highest loss in a single action of any Union regiment in the war.

*A*s their gunboat was preparing to go into action, a Union naval officer asked a sailor why he was on his knees, to which the youthful tar replied, "Praying, sir, that the enemy's bullets may be distributed the same way as the prize money, principally among the officers."

*T*he death of Stonewall Jackson inspired at least 47 poems and musical odes.

★ ★ ★

*E*arly on the morning of 2 July 1863—the second day of Gettysburg—Robert E. Lee conferred with several of his generals in the Adams County Prison, on High Street in Gettysburg, which is now a library.

★ ★ ★

*D*uring the battle of Chickamauga (19-20 September 1863) an Irishman in the Confederate 10th Tennessee refused to take up the colors, because, "By the holy Saint Patrick, Colonel, there's so much good shooting here, I haven't a minute's time to waste fooling with that thing."

★ ★ ★

*C*laiming that Brig. Gen. Lucius M. Walker had failed to render his division proper support during the Confederate retreat from Helena, Arkansas, on 4 July 1863, Brig. Gen. John S. Marmaduke challenged him to a duel, so that, the following September, he had the satisfaction of cutting down his comrade-in-arms in properly genteel fashion, with a slug through the body.

★ ★ ★

A Union army corps of 11,000 men occupied only three miles of road if the troops marched four abreast and it proceeded without artillery or impedimenta, but, fully 18 miles when the 225 wagons, 26 artillery equipments, 50 ambulances, and various other vehicles were included.

*T*he Union and the Confederacy each lost five generals in action at Gettysburg.

A gentleman who called upon Lincoln to request a pass through the lines to Richmond was told, "Well, I would be very happy to oblige you, if my passes were respected; but the fact is, sir, I have, within the last two years, given passes to 250,000 men to go to Richmond, and not one has got there yet."

*O*n 16 July 1863, as the Republic basked in the aftermath of its victories at Gettysburg, Vicksburg, and Tullahoma, it was achieving yet another success, in far-off Japan, where the six-gun U.S.S. *Wyoming* sank two vessels, damaged a third, and shot up shore installations in the Shimonoseki Straits, in retaliation for an attack by the Choshiu Clan on an American merchant ship.

*A*lthough cut off in the midst of the enemy as a result of the Union retreat on the first day of Gettysburg, Brig. Gen. Alexander Schimmelfennig managed to preserve his freedom—if not his dignity—until the Confederates evacuated the town three days later by hiding in a pig sty.

*I*n April of 1863 Robert E. Ford, the clerk of the *Journal* of the Confederate House of Representatives, killed Robert S. Dixon, the chief clerk of the House, in a shoot-out in Richmond's Capitol Square, because the latter had criticized him for carelessness in the execution of his duties.

*W*hen, after days of hard fighting at Stone's River/Murfreesboro (31 December 1862 to 2 January 1863), the Confederates began to retreat, a soldier of the *64th Ohio* began to sing "Praise God, From Whom All Blessings Flow," which was soon taken up by the rest of the regiment and then by much of the Union army as well.

*D*uring fiscal year 1862-1863, 338,000,000 tons of military stores were transported by river for the Union armies in the Western Theater, as against only 153,100,000 by rail.

★ ★ ★

*T*he only occasion during the war on which Lee actually showed himself to be angry was on the morning of the third day of Gettysburg, when he was seen to raise his hand as if to strike J.E.B. Stuart, who had finally turned up after being out of communication for several days on one of his rides around the Union army, leaving Lee to operate in an intelligence vacuum.

*T*here were 39 Missouri regiments at the siege of Vicksburg, 22 in blue and 17 in gray.

*I*nformed by a medium that a distinguished Indian chief in the next world wished to speak with him, Lincoln is said to have replied, "I should be happy to hear what his Indian majesty has to say. We have recently had a visitation from our red brethren, and it was the only delegation, black, white, or blue, which did not volunteer some advice about the conduct of the war."

*W*hen, on the afternoon of the second day at Gettysburg, some troops cheered him as they prepared to go into action, Confederate Lt. Gen. James Longstreet replied, "Cheer less, men, fight more!"

*F*rom March through October of 1863 the 36 cavalry regiments in the *Army of the Potomac* required 35,380 remounts, or roughly 2.5 per trooper.

★ ★ ★

*W*hen, in March of 1863, U.S. Grant attempted to reroute the Mississippi River with a canal across the DeSoto Peninsula in order to leave Vicksburg high and dry, he was unaware that the trick had already been attempted by the state of Louisiana some years before the war, in the hope that it might profit from its sister state's loss.

★ ★ ★

*A*dmonished by a preacher to the effect that Satan was the true enemy, not the Rebels, a wounded Union soldier replied, "Satan is a pretty bad fellow, but he can't give us worse than we got at Chickamauga."

★ ★ ★

*A*s a result of an argument over whose battery had precedence on the line of march, Capt. Pichegru Woolfolk, Jr., of Virginia's Ashlad Battery, was challenged to a duel with rifles at 15 paces by Capt. George W. Moody, of Louisiana's Madison Light Artillery, but the expected encounter never took place, the battle of Gettysburg interfering in the arrangements and, although both survived, neither ever met the other again.

★ ★ ★

Confederate Maj. Gen. Sterling Price once had to lecture his men about the Crusades before he could get them to use new battleflags decorated with red crosses, for the staunchly Protestant troops suspected a Catholic plot.

In a moment of panic about the supply of horseflesh during the summer of 1863, Union Secretary of War Edwin M. Stanton proposed mounting some cavalrymen on mules.

At dawn on 21 August 1863, a day which Jefferson Davis had proclaimed to be one of "fasting, humiliation, and prayer" throughout the South, Col. William C. Quantrill rode into Lawrence, Kansas, with 450 men and proceeded to murder 150 men and boys in the name of the Confederacy.

At Gettysburg over a third of the *Army of the Potomac* was composed of Pennsylvania men, including their commander, Maj. Gen. George Meade, who, as Lincoln had predicted, fought well "for his own dung heap."

*S*o impressed was Union Col. John T. Wilder by the new Spencer repeating rifles that, when the War Department refused to issue them to his troops, he convinced the men of his command to pledge $35 apiece, stood surety for a note to cover the costs, and went out and bought several thousand, so that his brigade became the first in history to be completely equipped with repeaters, with devastating effect in action.

*F*ederal gunners fired 32,781 artillery rounds at Gettysburg.

*C*onfederate Maj. Gen. Earl Van Dorn came to an unusual end for a Civil War general when, on 7 May 1863 one Dr. Peters shot him in the back because he had "violated the sanctity of his home" by seducing his wife, a charge which the general's friends denied, but which was probably true.

A number of men who wished to join the *16th New York Caualry* (the *Sprague Light Cavalry*) were not permitted to do so because they failed to realize that the phrase "men allowed to furnish their own horses" meant "bring your own."

Among the Russian naval officers wintering in New York in 1863-1864—the Tsar wanted his fleet far away should he get into war with Britain and France—was one who would later become famous, Nikolai Andreevich Rimsky-Korsakov, who spent part of the time writing a symphony in E flat minor.

Mrs. Ora Palmer of North Carolina lost all four of her sons in the battle of Gettysburg.

★ ★ ★

Once, when a soldier's application for furlough had been denied by a lower commander, Confederate Maj. Gen. D.H. Hill reversed the decision on the grounds that "a brave soldier ought to be allowed to go home whenever practicable, otherwise the children born during the war or within the usual period afterwards will be the off-spring of the cowards who remain at home."

★ ★ ★

When Pickett's Charge had been beaten off on the third day of Gettysburg, Union Col. Arthur F. Devereaux of the *19th Massachusetts* was found to have four Confederate colors draped over his arm.

*A*t one point in the war the Yankee *7th Tennessee* was captured by the Rebel *7th Tennessee.*

★ ★ ★

*W*hen, late in 1863, some Mississippi troops announced that, their enlistment being up, they were going home, Confederate Maj. Gen. Sterling Price convinced them to re-up by calling out, "All of you who want to re-enlist step forward; all of you who want to be shot, stand still."

★ ★ ★

*D*uring a raid into a Rebel-held area of eastern Virginia during December of 1863, a black infantry regiment marched 60 miles in 40 hours, a feat rivaling that of "Jackson's Foot Cavalry" at its best.

1864

*W*hen John G. Nicolay, Lincoln's secretary, was drafted in 1864, he hired a substitute, Hiram Child, a black man from North Carolina who was later killed in action.

★ ★ ★

*O*n separate occasions during 1864, Episcopal Bishop and Confederate Lt. Gen. Leonidas Polk baptized Joseph E. Johnston and John B. Hood, setting some sort of a record, in as much as both of these gentlemen were full generals.

★ ★ ★

*D*uring Confederate Gen. John B. Hood's offensive in 1864 the Union Army confiscated over 7,000 horses in Kentucky and Tennessee, including a team of coach horses belonging to Andrew Johnson, who was at the time the vice-president elect of the United States.

★ ★ ★

*C*oming upon the mansion of a woman he had once courted, Sherman put the place under guard and left a message for his erstwhile sweetheart which read "You once said that you would pity the man who would ever become my enemy. My answer was that I would ever protect and shield you. This I have done. Forgive me all else. I am but a soldier."

★ ★ ★

*M*rs. Lincoln's closest confidant during the war, and her principal comfort on the death of the president, was Mrs. Elizabeth Keckley, a black seamstress, who had once been employed by Mrs. Davis.

★ ★ ★

*I*n a demonstration of what the war was all about, at Saltville, Virginia, on 2 October 1864, Confederate troops murdered about 100 black prisoners-of-war from the *5th* and *6th United States Colored Cavalry.*

★ ★ ★

*W*hen, during the battle of Mobile Bay (5 August 1864), the wooden U.S.S. *Lakawanna* rammed the Confederacy's *Tennessee* with little effect save to herself, several crewmen of the rebel ironclad stuck their heads out of her gun ports and addressed "opprobrious language" at the Yankee vessel, whereupon the latter's marines drove them back with a shower of holystones and spitoons, liberally seasoned with some musket balls.

★ ★ ★

*T*he price of a 15-inch 320-pounder Rodman muzzle-loading naval gun was $7,000, at a time when $250 a year was a good income for a laborer.

★ ★ ★

*W*hen Cpl. Mike Scannel of the *19th Massachusetts* displayed some reluctance to carry the flag at Cold Harbor, his regimental commander said, "I'll make you a sergeant on the spot!" to which Scannel replied, "That's business," grabbed the colors, and led the troops forward.

★ ★ ★

*T*he principal victim of a Confederate plot to put New York City to the torch on 25 November 1864 was P.T. Barnum's Museum, which burned spectacularly and proved a total loss, including the Egress.

★ ★ ★

*W*hile visiting a regiment which had not been paid for some time, newly appointed Chief Justice Salmon P. Chase—whose portrait graced the $20 greenback—chanced upon an old acquaintance who at first did not seem to recognize him, later explaining, "It is so long since we have seen your picture that I had almost forgotten you."

★ ★ ★

*I*n January of 1864 Union Brig. Gen. John Beatty resigned his commission in order to go home and relieve his brother of the burden of running the family business, so that the latter could have a taste of military life.

★ ★ ★

*F*inding himself unemployed and in a bad odor as a result of having surrendered Vicksburg, Confederate Lt. Gen. John C. Pemberton resigned his Provisional Army commission in 1864 to resume his Regular Army rank of a lieutenant colonel of artillery, as which he served for the balance of the war.

★ ★ ★

*D*uring the battle of Kennesaw Mountain (27 June 1864), a small woods in which some Union wounded were sheltering caught fire, whereupon Confederate Col. W.H. Martin of the *1st Arkansas* jumped up on a parapet, waved a white flag, and shouted, "We won't fire until you get them away," with the result that a brief truce occurred while the Union wounded were evacuated, at the end of which a Yankee major gave Martin a brace of pistols in gratitude for his brave and gallant gesture.

★ ★ ★

U.S. Grant apparently smoked about two dozen cigars a day.

★ ★ ★

*A*t Sand Creek, Colorado Territory, on 29 November 1864, the *3rd Colorado Volunteer Cavalry,* under the command of Col. John Milton Chivington, a Methodist minister and elder, massacred an entire village of Cheyenne who were at the time under the protection of the United States of America.

★ ★ ★

*C*onfederate cavalrymen had to provide their own horses, and, although the army reimbursed them if their mounts died as a result of combat, they received nothing if the beast died of overwork or illness.

*A*t the battle of the Opequon (13 September 1864), some of Confederate Lt. Gen. Jubal Early's infantry formed square to meet the charge of five of Union Maj. Gen. Philip Sheridan's cavalry brigades, one of the few instances in the Civil War of this tactic being used.

★ ★ ★

*I*n January of 1864 over 136,000 time-expired Union veterans reenlisted, amounting to about 16 percent of the men under arms at the time.

★ ★ ★

*C*aptured at Plymouth, North Carolina, on 20 April 1864, the *85th New York* lost 222 men in Confederate prisoner-of-war camps.

★ ★ ★

*D*uring the Atlanta campaign, Union engineers erected an 800-foot-long, 100-foot-high railroad bridge over the Chattahoochee River in 4.5 days, from standing timber to first train.

★ ★ ★

*W*hile touring the trenches at Petersburg one day, Gen. Robert E. Lee found that Brig. Gen. Archibald Gracie, Jr. appeared to be obscuring his view as he indicated points of interest in the Yankee lines, and so remarked "General, you should not expose yourself so much," to which Gracie—who was trying to shield Lee from Union marksmen—replied, "If *I* should not, General Lee, why should you?" at which Lee smiled and retired to a less exposed position.

*F*ully 129 (30.6 percent) of the 425 Confederate generals, and 126 (21.6 percent) of the 583 Union generals, had been lawyers before the war.

*I*n late 1864 the *1st Wisconsin Heavy Artillery* did an unusual thing: it elected Ella H. Gibson as chaplain, in which post she served to the satisfaction of all concerned until the end of the war.

★ ★ ★

Confederate Brig. Gen. William N.R. Beall, who was captured in July of 1863, had perhaps the most unusual imprisonment of the war: released on parole, he spent over a year in an office in New York City supervising the procurement of supplies for Confederates held as prisoners-of-war, with funds provided by the sale of cotton which was passed through the lines under a special convention.

Confederate Col. George S. Patton, who fell at the head of the 22nd Virginia at Winchester on 19 September 1864, had a grandson who later attained some distinction as a soldier.

The 5,597 Union dead in the battle of the Wilderness (5-7 May 1864) exceeded the combined American battle deaths of both the War of 1812 (2,260) and the Mexican War (1,733), which together lasted nearly five years.

During a debate on the floor of the Senate of the Confederate States of America in late 1864, the Honorable Senator Benjamin H. Hill of Georgia demonstrated the strength of his argument to the Honorable Senator William L. Yancey of Alabama by striking him in the face with an inkwell.

Corruption aside, one reason that Union authorities tolerated an extraordinary amount of covert commerce with the Confederacy was that many of the smugglers were Federal intelligence agents.

At one point during Sherman's Georgia campaign Rebel pickets lacking entrenching tools borrowed them from their Yankee counterparts.

The Chimborazo Military Hospital in Richmond was the largest medical facility in the world, capable of handling 4,800 cases simultaneously with 150 ward buildings, kitchens, a bakery, dairy herd, an ice house, and various other facilities spread over 125 acres.

Col. Daniel McCook, Jr.—one of the 17 "Fighting McCooks of Ohio"—recited several verses from Macaulay's "Horatius at the Bridge," beginning with "And how can men die better than facing fearful odds. . . ?" as he led his brigade into action at Kennesaw Mountain on 27 June 1864, where he was mortally wounded.

Confederate soldiers claimed that of the $301 paid to their generals, only $1.00 was for services rendered, with the rest "thrown in to please them."

★ ★ ★

At the peak of the war the defenses of Washington included 807 guns and 98 mortars, distributed among some 75 forts and batteries.

★ ★ ★

While on a riverine expedition in search of Rebels and cotton—not necessarily in that order—Union Rear Adm. David Dixon Porter remarked, "Armies loot, navies take prizes."

★ ★ ★

On 7 May 1864 the men of the veteran *3rd Pennsylvania Cavalry* arranged to exchange their worn-out mounts for fresher ones, a matter which held up the advance of the *Army of the Potomac* for about two hours, since the green regiment which possessed the animals proved loath to part with them.

★ ★ ★

Robert E. Lee's spartan tastes were such that Richard Taylor once remarked, "General Lee was never so uncomfortable as when he was comfortable."

★ ★ ★

*A*s the Federal monitor *Tecumseh* was sinking after being mined in Mobile Bay on 8 May 1864, her skipper, the courteous Cdr. T.A.M. Craven, politely stepped aside to let the steersman escape first, and so went down with the ship, which foundered in about 90 seconds.

*I*n the course of the war the Union "recruited" some 825,000 horses and 450,000 mules.

*D*isapproving a musician's request for leave, Confederate Maj. Gen. D.H. Hill explained that priority for leave was for "shooters, not tooters."

*B*y 1864 a recruit could receive $677 if he enlisted in New York City—$302 from the Federal government, $75 from the state, and $300 from the city—and if he were a veteran, another $100 on top of that, for a total of $777, and some manpower-poor communities paid as much as double that sum.

*D*uring the long siege of Petersburg in 1864–1865 it was not uncommon for troops to slip across the lines for a poker game in the enemy trenches.

*I*t has been estimated that on the average a mounted officer was hit once for every four horses which were shot out from under him.

★ ★ ★

*M*aj. Gen. "Uncle" John Sedgwick, the oldest corps commander in the *Army of the Potomac* was so well-liked that when he was killed in action on 9 May 1864, U.S. Grant was so stunned as to twice ask, "Is he really dead?"

★ ★ ★

*T*he desertion rate among black troops in the Union Army was only about 60 percent that of white troops.

★ ★ ★

*A*rriving early and in mufti for an appointment with a lady whom he had not previously met, John C. Breckinridge was asked for three references, to which he replied, "Former Vice-President of the United States, former United States Senator, and Major General, Provisional Army of the Confederate States of America," whereupon his embarrassed hostess explained that he had been mistaken for an applicant for employment as a footman.

★ ★ ★

So confused were the lines during the battle of the Wilderness that at one point a group of Federal infantrymen blundered into a group of Confederates and, thinking themselves outgunned, quickly fell back, thereby missing a chance to bag Robert E. Lee, A.P. Hill, and J.E.B. Stuart, who were conferring with their staffs.

When in June of 1864, Union Maj. Gen. David Hunter's troops passed Stonewall Jackson's grave in Lexington, Virginia, they halted, removed their caps, and then, after a moment's pause, marched off.

According to one musically inclined Union infantryman serving with the *Army of the Potomac,* as a minie ball passed overhead one heard "a swell from E flat to F, and as it passed into the distance and lost its velocity, receded to D—a pretty change."

Union Maj. Gen. William T. Sherman estimated that his "March to the Sea" inflicted $100,000,000 worth of damage on Georgia, of which only about a quarter was "useful to the army."

The American Bible Society distributed 800,000 Bibles to the troops during the war, including—in a rare apolitical gesture—over 100,000 to Confederate soldiers.

★ ★ ★

The greatest infantry attack of the war was not Pickett's Charge at Gettysburg on 3 July 1863, but rather that of Confederate Gen. John B. Hood's *Army of Tennessee* at the battle of Franklin on 30 November 1864, when 20,000 men attacked across 2 miles of open ground, being beaten off in little more than an hour with over 6,000 casualties, including 6 generals killed, 5 wounded, and 1 captured, proportionally a greater loss than in any other such attack of the war, though Union Lt. Gen. U.S. Grant's attack at Cold Harbor on 3 June 1864, which saw 40,000 men make a close assault against a virtually impregnable position with over 7,000 casualties in but half an hour, incurred greater losses in a far shorter period.

★ ★ ★

The most successful Confederate blockade runner was a ship named *Hattie,* which made more than 60 trips through the Union fleet, over 50 percent more than any other vessel.

★ ★ ★

A Federal remount station at Giesboro, on the Potomac near Washington, covered 625 acres, with complete facilities to accommodate 30,000 horses, including 2,500 in hospital.

★ ★ ★

*C*onfederate Lt. Gen. J.E.B. Stuart wore a beard because he had a "short and retiring" chin described by some as "girlish," which at West Point had earned him the nickname "Beauty."

★ ★ ★

*W*hen, on 17 May 1864, Confederate Maj. Gen. George Pickett's wife gave birth to their first child, U.S. Grant ordered celebratory fires lit along the front to match those built by Pickett's men, and, a few days later, sent the little one some silver spoons as a gift.

★ ★ ★

*S*ince both the Union and Confederate armies relied heavily upon horse transport, at any given time for every three animals used by the cavalry, artillery, or supply columns, an additional pair were required each week merely to transport fodder.

★ ★ ★

*A*t the height of the war about 90,000 letters passed through Washington each day and another 90,000 through Louisville, all bound to or from Union troops in the field.

One of Sherman's regiments was so good at foraging that it was said to be able to catch, scrape, and skin a hog without a soldier leaving the ranks.

★ ★ ★

Having lost an election bet, Nevada merchant R.C. Gridley toted a 20-pound sack of flour a mile through the town of Austin and then, inspired to do something for the war effort, sold it at auction and donated the proceeds to the United States Sanitary Commission, an act which the buyer repeated, as did each subsequent purchaser, so that over $70,000 was eventually raised.

★ ★ ★

Upon seeing for the first time the headquarters flag of the *Army of the Potomac,* a large, swallow-tailed affair with a golden eagle within a silver wreath on a solferino—fuscian red—field, U.S. Grant remarked, "What's this? Is Imperial Caesar somewhere about here?"

★ ★ ★

When Sherman ordered the population of Atlanta to leave the city in late 1864, there were only about 1,500 people still living there, the rest having already pulled out.

★ ★ ★

The biggest "jump" in rank ever awarded in the Confederate Army went to 27-year-old Capt. Victor J.B. Girardey, whom Lee promoted to brigadier general on 30 June 1864, as a result of his heroic service during the battle of the Crater: Brig. Gen Girardey was killed soon after, on 16 August.

Bakeries established by the Union Army at City Point, Virginia, in mid-1864 had a daily capacity of 123,000 loaves of "soft tack."

One day three shabbily dressed little girls strayed into the White House during a reception, wandered around a bit, and, coming upon the president, attempted to leave, whereupon he said, "Little girls! Are you going to pass me without shaking hands?" and proceeded to bend his awkward form down to their level and solemnly shook each one by the hand.

Union Chaplain Milton Haney of the *55th Illinois* won the Medal of Honor before Atlanta on 22 July 1864 when he led a counterattack which retook some trenches from the enemy after the death of Maj. Gen. James B. McPherson.

*A*s a captured Rebel was being taken past a Union artillery park just outside the Petersburg lines in Virginia, he is said to have remarked, "By God, you fellers have almost as many guns marked 'U.S.' as we do."

★ ★ ★

*D*uring the war many soldiers had a "house-wife"—a small sewing and grooming kit-provided in hundreds of thousands by mothers, wives, sweethearts, sisters, daughters, or the Soldier's Aid Society.

★ ★ ★

*T*rying to stem the rout after the collapse of Confederate Gen. John B. Hood's attack at Ezra Church, near Atlanta, on 28 July 1864, an officer shouted, "What are you running for?" to which one soldier replied, "Bekase I kaint fly!"

★ ★ ★

*O*ne day, just as he was getting ready to advance on Richmond, U.S. Grant was asked how long it would take him to get the Confederate capitol, to which he replied, "I will agree to be there in about four days, that is, if General Lee becomes a party to the agreement, but if he objects, the trip will undoubtedly be prolonged."

★ ★ ★

*T*he only living person ever honored on an American postage stamp was Jefferson Davis.

*D*uring his "March to the Sea" Maj. Gen. William T. Sherman gave instructions to a division commander to follow a particular line of march, admonishing him to keep in close communication, and adding, as he rode away, "See here, Cox, burn a few barns occasionally, as you go along. I can't understand those signal flags, but I know what smoke means."

★ ★ ★

U.S. Grant must have found the Wilderness campaign a particularly trying time, for during it he was several times heard to say "Confound it!" and "Doggone it!" though he had heretofore never been heard to utter even the mildest oath.

★ ★ ★

*B*y the end of 1864 many Confederate regiments were mere skeletons: in the *Army of Tennessee*, the *3rd* and *18th Tennessee* together amounted to a dozen men.

1865

The town of Winchester, in Virginia's strategically important Shenandoah Valley, changed hands 76 times during the course of the Civil War.

★ ★ ★

A mathematics book published in the South during the war included the problem, "If one Confederate soldier can whip 7 Yankees, how many Confederate soldiers can whip 49 Yankees?"

★ ★ ★

There were 20 generals named Smith in the Civil War, twelve of whom wore blue and eight gray, making it the most common name for a general, being borne by 1.98 percent of the 1,008 generals.

★ ★ ★

The Confederacy expended about $2.1 billion on the war, roughly the value of human beings held in slavery in 1861.

Marcellus M. Crocker, one of the finer young Union generals—he was born in 1830—was distinguished not only for the skill and dash with which he led various brigades and divisions, but also because he never missed a battle due to illness, despite the fact that he had consumption when he volunteered and died of the disease within a few weeks of the end of the war.

★ ★ ★

Resistance to conscription was so strong in the Confederacy that by the war's end the Conscription Bureau had suffered 38 dead and 60 wounded, casualties greater than those incurred by some regiments.

★ ★ ★

At one point during the Carolina campaign Union Maj. Gen. Judson Kilpatrick was forced to flee in his drawers when his headquarters was surprised by some of Wade Hampton's cavalry while he was "entertaining" a sympathetic southern belle.

★ ★ ★

During the war the United States spent approximately $124 million on horses.

*T*he last Confederate general to lay down his arms was Brig. Gen. Stand Watie, a chief of the Cherokee nation, who did so on 23 June 1865, at Doaksville, in the Indian Territory, later Oklahoma.

*S*tatistically, an average of one man was killed or mortally wounded for every 4.8 men who suffered wounds less than mortal during the war.

*U*nion Brig. Gen. Alexander Schimmelfennig had the longest family name of any general in the war, with 13 letters; nosing out both the Confederacy's Maj. Gen. John C. Breckinridge and the Union's Maj. Gen. Samuel P. Heintzelman by one letter: the record for the shortest surname is tied among a half-dozen Confederates named Lee—four of whom were members of Robert E. Lee's family —plus two Union officers, Brig. Gen. Albert L. Lee and Maj. Gen. Edward O.C. Ord.

*D*uring the Civil War the Union Army issued about 4 million muskets, rifles, carbines, and the like, but only 7,892 pieces of artillery.

On 26 March 1865, Lincoln—who had just received word that the Confederacy had authorized the recruitment of black troops—was reviewing elements of the *Army of the James* when a black division marched by "well-aligned and keeping good step to the music," whereupon he remarked, "I wonder how Jeff Davis would like to have such colored troops in his army?"

Kansas probably holds the distinction of providing proportionally the greatest number of soldiers in the war, 18.8 percent of the state's 106,000 people serving, virtually all of them in blue.

Not once during the war was Abraham Lincoln heard to use the term "the enemy."

The *55th Illinois* was probably the most traveled regiment in the war, covering 11,965 miles by rail, steamboat, and foot, from the time it mustered into service at Chicago until the Grand Review in Washington nearly four years later.

Harvard lost 202 alumni during the Civil War, of whom 138 died for the Union and 64 for the Confederacy.

*T*he Union monitor *Comanche,* which was commissioned at San Francisco in January of 1865, had been built at Jersey City in 1863, where she was disassembled on the ways, and sent around the Horn aboard the merchantman *Aquila,* which foundered upon reaching San Francisco in November; salvaged, *Comanche* was reassembled and launched in November of 1864, a year after she had sunk.

*B*y the end of the war the town of Galena, Illinois, with but 15,000 inhabitants, had contributed 14 generals and field officers to the Union cause, including U.S. Grant.

*C*onfederate Brig. Gen. James Dearing was mostly wounded in an exchange of pistol shots with a Union officer whom he slew on 6 April 1865, during the retreat to Appomattox, but lingered on long enough to be paroled by his former West Point classmate, Union Brig. Gen. Ranald S. Mackenzie, shortly thereafter becoming the last Confederate general to die in the war, succumbing on 23 April.

*O*ne out of nine men in the Union armies died in the service, but only one in 56 died of wounds and one in 65 was killed in action.

*I*n a remarkable feat of improvisation, the Confederate Navy completed about 14 of the approximately 25 ironclad warships which it commenced to build, out of about 50 which it planned.

*S*tatistically, for every 1000 volunteers on the rolls of the Union Army at the beginning of each year, 75.4 died—45.3 by disease, 18.9 killed in action, and 11.2 of wounds—and 1.4 were missing in action, while 6.57 deserted, 90.7 received a medical discharge, and 66.2 were otherwise discharged, retired, or separated from the service each year, leaving only 761.13 men at the end of that year.

*A*s a result of an administrative foul-up late in the war, the Confederate Conscription Bureau once drafted a bed-ridden, dying 65-year-old man.

*I*n February of 1865 Mr. Kirk B. Wells of Philadelphia, who chanced to be visiting the *Army of the James* when an execution for desertion was being held, found his interest in observing the activity wane upon his discovery that the man to be shot was the one whom he had hired as a substitute.

*T*he record for number of generals in one family—including first cousins—is tied between the Union's "Fighting McCooks" of Ohio and the Confederacy's Lees of Virginia, with four each, though one might also include the three Ewing brothers of Ohio, whose foster brother and brother-in-law William T. Sherman was also a general.

*D*uring the Civil War the Union artillery fired approximately 5,000,000 rounds, or about four rounds per tube per day.

*A*lthough many more are known to have worn them at least some of the time, of 583 Union and 425 Confederate generals, only five— Yankees all and none of them notable—ever permitted themselves to be photographed wearing "spectacles."

*G*eorge B. Mattoon enlisted in the *1st New Hampshire Cavalry* in 1862 at the age of 15 and, when mustered out at the end of the war, was a veteran of some 70 battles and skirmishes, during which he was never once wounded, despite having two horses shot out from under him.

*W*hile brevet promotions to brigadier general were fairly common at the end of the Civil War, that awarded to Col. William M. Graham on 13 March 1865 must surely have been the most unusual, since he had died at the head of the old *11th Infantry* during the battle of Molino del Rey in Mexico on 8 September 1847.

*I*n an effort to ensure an adequate food supply, during the war six Confederate states— Virginia, the Carolinas, Georgia, Alabama, and Arkansas—enacted legislation prohibiting the distillation of grain into alcohol.

*O*n 21 February 1865 Union Maj. Gen. George Crook was captured by a band of Confederate partisan rangers while visiting his fiance, Mary Dailey, in Cumberland, Maryland, the raiders having been guided to the Dailey home by Miss Dailey's brother, one of their number.

*A*mong the 27 ships which the United States Navy lost to Confederate submarine mines—"torpedoes"—during the war, were four monitors and three ironclad gunboats.

*W*hen Abraham Lincoln's body was returned to Springfield, Illinois, in 1865, it was accompanied by Maj. Gen. David Hunter, who as a major in 1861 had accompanied Lincoln on his journey from Springfield to Washington.

★　★　★

*T*he standard gunpowder formula used by both sides during the Civil War was 76 percent nitre, 14 percent willow or poplar charcoal, and 10 percent sulphur, which burns somewhat more rapidly, and with somewhat more smoke and slightly less power than the optimal formula, 74.64 percent nitre, 13.51 percent charcoal, and 11.85 percent sulphur.

★　★　★

*A*lthough their numbers are unknown, the Civil War was apparently the first in which Chinese-Americans saw military service.

★　★　★

*N*ew York City contributed 809 companies of infantry, 114 of cavalry, 65 of artillery, and 18 of engineers to the Union war effort.

★　★　★

*B*rig. Gen. William H. Pendleton, the chief of artillery of the Army of Northern Virginia, was an ordained minister who conducted regular Sunday services and numberless prayer meetings throughout the war.

★　★　★

*A*ltogether about 18 percent of Confederate manpower, but only 6 percent of Union manpower, was supplied through the draft, in the form of conscripts or substitutes.

★ ★ ★

*A*ndrew A. Humphreys, who rose to a major generalcy in the Union Army, could have done nought else, for his father and grandfather had designed the famed frigate U.S.S. *Constitution*.

★ ★ ★

*R*ural areas and small towns provided 78 percent of the generals in the war, a figure roughly proportional to that for the troops.

★ ★ ★

*B*rig. Gen. Thomas A. Smyth, who was mortally wounded during the Appomattox campaign on 7 April 1865, died two days later, the last Union general to be killed in the war.

★ ★ ★

*D*uring the war the venereal disease rate among Union troops was 8.2 percent: there were a reported 79,587 cases of syphilis and 102,873 of gonorrhea.

★ ★ ★

*A*fter winning the last battle of the war, at Palmetto Ranch, Texas, on 12 May 1865, Confederate Brig. Gen. James E. Slaughter withdrew his forces across the Rio Grande and sold his artillery to the Imperial Mexican Maj. Gen. Tomas Meija for $20,000 in gold.

★ ★ ★

*A*braham Lincoln served as president of the United States for 1,503 days.

★ ★ ★

*T*he highest ranking Native American in the war was the Cherokee chief Degataga, known to the whites as Stand Watie, who became a Confederate brigadier general and commanded a brigade of his brethren in the Trans-Mississippi theater; the highest ranking Indian in the Union Army was the Seneca sachem Donehogawa, Ely S. Parker, a colonel and brigadier general by brevet, who served as Grant's military secretary, recording the terms of Lee's surrender at Appomattox.

★ ★ ★

*I*n the last two years of the war about 30 percent of Union manpower was engaged in guarding lines of communication and supply from raids by Confederate cavalry and guerrillas.

★ ★ ★

*A*lthough they performed all the functions of a government, and although they waged war with considerable skill and remarkable success for over four years, the group of Southern states which attempted to secede from the Union in 1861 never had a name, the form "The Confederate States of America" which appeared on currency, laws, military regulations, and passports, never officially having been adopted.

★ ★ ★

*T*he United States procured over 1,250,000,000 percussion caps during the war.

★ ★ ★

*U*pon hearing the news of the assassination of Lincoln, Confederate Lt. Gen. Richard S. Ewell, who was a prisoner-of-war at the time, is said to have burst into tears.

★ ★ ★

*T*he last men to join the Confederacy were eight seamen who signed on aboard the raider C.S.S. *Shenandoah* on 28 June 1865, five days *after* the last Confederate general had laid down his arms.

★ ★ ★

The names of two Civil War generals seem to have determined the side on which they fought: Confederate Brig. Gen. States Rights Gist and Union Brig. Gen. Thomas Wilberforce Egan, named after the pioneering Abolitionist William Wilberforce.

Between 8,000 and 10,000 Jewish Americans served in the Union Army and perhaps 2,000 in the Confederate, out of a population of no more than 150,000.

Confederate Brig. Gen. William Smith was—barring the great Stonewall—perhaps the most eccentric general in the war; in at least one battle he fought wearing an old beaver "stove pipe" hat and, since the weather was threatening, toting an umbrella.

Railroad mileage in the United States increased by almost 13 percent during the Civil War, despite the destruction of many of the lines in the South.

Only one of the 25 highest ranking Confederate generals had not received the benefits of a higher education, Nathan Bedford Forrest.

*D*uring the war the Union forces consumed about 50 percent of the North's industrial production.

★ ★ ★

*W*hen some of his men cheered news of Lincoln's assassination, Confederate Gen. Pierre G.T. Beauregard became noticeably angry for the first time in the war, shouting, "Shut those men up. If they don't shut up have them arrested."

★ ★ ★

*B*y 1865 the Union was expending $4,000,000 a day on the war.

★ ★ ★

*R*obert E. Lee and Jerome B. Robertson were the only Confederate generals to have sons who were also Confederate generals; no Union general was the father of another Union general, although Pennsylvania state militia Maj. Gen. Robert Patterson's son Francis E. Patterson became a brigadier general and Union Brig. Gen. Philip St. George Cooke was the father of Confederate Brig. Gen. John R. Cooke.

★ ★ ★

*T*hough figures are difficult to reconcile and compare, about 12 percent of the white population of the Union served in the war, compared with roughly 17 percent of the white population of the Confederacy; about 6 percent of the black population of the nation served in arms, and many more as laborers on both sides.

★ ★ ★

*O*ver 5,000,000 acres of public land were transferred to private ownership during the Civil War, much of it under the terms of the "Homestead Act" of 1862.

★ ★ ★

*C*onfederate Lt. Gen. Nathan Bedford Forrest lost 29 horses shot out from under him during the war, probably a world's record.

★ ★ ★

*T*he cost of Civil War, $3,200,000,000, amounted to over $800 for each of the 3,935,760 people held as slaves in the country in 1860, which was nearly twice their average market value, and that figure excludes the loss of life and property, Confederate expenditures, and the enormous pension burden which the war created.

★ ★ ★

*D*uring the war Union prisoner-of-war camps had a mortality rate of about 12 percent, Confederate ones of about 15.5 percent.

The last time Abraham "The Railsplitter" Lincoln wielded an axe was during his final visit to the *Army of the Potomac,* shortly before the fall of Richmond, when he gave a demonstration of the presidential technique which resulted in his "making the chips fly" and leaving "as smooth a cut as the best lumberman in Maine could do," a feat which elicited cheers from the troops.

About 150,000 Confederate soldiers were baptized during the war, including a half-dozen generals.

When the last brigade of the Army of Northern Virginia completed laying down its arms at Appomattox, the escorting Union troops, hitherto silent, are said to have offered three lusty cheers for the Rebels.

Although one was constitutionally provided for, the Confederacy never got around to establishing a Supreme Court.

★ ★ ★

*A*bout 24 percent of the 29,980 amputations performed by Union Army surgeons during the Civil War had fatal consequences, a figure greatly exceeded during the Franco-Prussian War, which broke out five years later, when 77 percent of the approximately 13,000 amputations performed by French Army surgeons resulted in death.

★　★　★

*D*uring the Civil War Robert E. Lee's hair turned from a strong black to completely white.

★　★　★

*F*ully 1,149 vessels were captured and sent to Admiralty courts by the Union Navy during the war, for a total prize value of nearly $25,000,000, all divided up among the officers and men of the capturing vessels: an additional 355 vessels worth about $7,000,000 were burned or otherwise destroyed.

★　★　★

*T*he number of civilian employees of the Federal government rose during the war from about 40,000 to about 105,000, or over 260 percent.

★　★　★

*W*hen the *20th Massachusetts* (*The Harvard Regiment*) mustered out after 4 years and 10 days of military service, only 2 of the original 34 officers were present for duty.

★ ★ ★

*C*onsidering both armies together, there were an estimated 1,700,000 cases of dysentery and 1,200,000 of malaria during the war.

★ ★ ★

*I*t is remarkable that, in a war in which politicking for promotion was commonplace, one Yankee and three Rebels actually declined generalships.

★ ★ ★

*O*nly 5 percent of the money expended on the war by the Confederacy was raised through taxation and a further 5 percent through miscellaneous fees and revenues, while 30 percent was provided from loans, and fully 60 percent by printing paper money, whereas the Union derived 4 percent from miscellaneous fees and revenues, 62 percent from loans, 21 percent from taxes, and only 13 percent by printing greenbacks.

★ ★ ★

*U*nion Maj. Gen. Godfrey Weitzel, initially one of the most outspoken opponents of the use of black troops, ended the war in command of the *XXV Army Corps,* a black outfit.

★ ★ ★

The Federal regiments which marched into Richmond on 3 April 1865 did so to the strains of "Dixie."

★ ★ ★

Five pairs of brothers received the Medal of Honor during the Civil War.

★ ★ ★

The greatest military parade in the history of the United States occurred in Washington on 23-24 May 1865, when about 150,000 veterans marched in the Grand Review of the Armies before President Andrew Johnson.

★ ★ ★

The $3,200,000,000 which the Union spent to fight the war amounted to about $126 per capita, or an estimated $115,200,000,000—about $4,500 apiece—in money of 1988.

★ ★ ★

West Point graduates and drop-outs accounted for 156 of the Confederacy's 425 generals (36.7 percent) and 228 of the Union's 583 generals (39.1 percent); in addition, one graduate of Annapolis became a Union general (.0017 percent).

★ ★ ★

The only Confederate vessel to circumnavigate the globe was the cruiser C.S.S. *Shenandoah*.

The worst hit Union regiment in the war was the *2nd Wisconsin*, which lost 19.7 percent of its wartime enrollment; the worst hit black regiment was the *79th U.S.C.T.*, which lost 15.0 percent of those enrolled.

★ ★ ★

Twenty Canadians were awarded the Medal of Honor during the war.

★ ★ ★

As a result of the depredations of Confederate commerce raiders, insurance rates for American flag vessels doubled during the war.

★ ★ ★

The Union's *Casco* class monitors were so badly designed that they could not be completed as intended; had their turrets been mounted they would have sunk.

★ ★ ★

On 28 April 1865 Union Col. Galusha Pennypacker was promoted to brigadier general, which was nice because it came shortly before his 21st birthday (1 June), making him the youngest general on either side in the war, and the only general in American history who was too young to vote.

★ ★ ★

*D*uring the Civil War eye injuries accounted for only .57 percent of the total number of wounds, roughly 10 percent of what the comparable figure is today.

★ ★ ★

*I*t is estimated that half of all rations procured for the Union forces during the war were lost due to improper storage, poor preparation, or carelessness, not to mention capture.

★ ★ ★

*O*f about 2,000 blockade runners active at various times during the war, fully 1,500 were eventually captured, and only about 150 remained active at the end of the fighting.

★ ★ ★

*A*t the Confederacy's Andersonville prison the death rate averaged 100 men each day.

★ ★ ★

*A*s Lt. Gen. U.S. Grant rode up to the McLean house in Appomattox on 9 April 1865 for his fateful meeting with Gen. Robert E. Lee, a Union Army band played "Auld Lang Syne."

★ ★ ★

*W*hile the two were alone together in a hotel room in Houston, Texas, on 6 April 1865, Confederate Col. George W. Baylor shot his unarmed superior, Maj. Gen. John A. Wharton.

*O*f 1,804 Union sailors and marines who died as a result of combat during the Civil War, 342 (18.96 percent) were scalded to death by steam escaping from boilers which had been pierced by enemy fire.

★ ★ ★

*A*n estimated 36,000 people were subject to various war-time abridgements of their civil rights in the North during the war, ranging from imprisonment without trial to less serious matters.

★ ★ ★

*A*t the height of the war the Union's Washington supply depot provided an average of 25,000 pairs of shoes a month to the armies.

★ ★ ★

*S*ince Confederate Gen. Pierre G.T. Beauregard had briefly served as a private in the Orleans Guard—the 13th Louisiana—at the start of the war, his name was ever afterwards included in roll calls, with the color sergeant replying, "Absent on duty."

★ ★ ★

*F*ewer than 1,000 of the 245,000 wounds treated in Union hospitals were inflicted by bayonets, less than .4 percent.

The most wounded general in the war was probably Confederate Brig. Gen. William R. Cox, who accumulated eleven wounds between April of 1861 and Appomattox, or roughly one every four months, a probable world's record.

★ ★ ★

Between 1861 and 1865 the number of horses engaged in agriculture in United States declined from 4,199,141 to 3,740,923, a drop of 12 percent.

★ ★ ★

There were three generals in the war named Winfield Scott, of whom the most distinguished was Union brevet Lt. Gen. Winfield Scott, hero of the War of 1812 and conqueror of Mexico, plus Union Maj. Gen. Winfield Scott Hancock and Confederate Brig. Gen. Winfield Scott Featherstone, who were named after him.

★ ★ ★

The flag which Union Maj. Gen. Robert Anderson hoisted over newly recaptured Fort Sumter on 14 April 1865 was that which he had been forced to lower on 14 April 1861.

★ ★ ★

Mrs. Polly Ray of North Carolina lost seven sons in the Confederate Army during the war.

*D*espite four years of strenuous diplomatic efforts, only one country extended recognition to the Confederacy, the tiny German Duchy of Saxe-Coburg-Gotha, and that because Duke Albrecht was married to an Alabama belle.

★ ★ ★

*T*here were officially 267 executions carried out by the Union Army during the war, plus an unknown number of unofficial ones.

★ ★ ★

*S*hortly after Confederate President Jefferson Davis was captured near Irwinsville, Georgia, on 10 June 1865, Union troops discovered the remnants of the Confederate treasury, which they promptly proceeded to divide up in order to stage what was undoubtedly the most high stakes poker game in history, at least on paper.

★ ★ ★

*P*erhaps as many as 300 boys of 13 or younger were enrolled in the Union ranks during the war.

*A*lthough Confederate commerce raiders captured or destroyed only 263 American flag merchant vessels totaling about 105,000 gross tons—some 5 percent of the pre-war merchant fleet—the threat which they posed resulted in the transfer of nearly 1,000 vessels totaling some 800,000 gross tons—nearly 40 percent of the prewar fleet—delivering a blow to the U.S. merchant marine from which it never fully recovered.

*T*he formal surrender of the Army of Northern Virginia was held on 12 April 1865 four years to the day after the firing on Fort Sumter.

*I*t is estimated that the Union naval blockade was run about 8,250 times.

*T*radition has it that despite a remarkable combat record, Union Col. Wladimir Krzyzanowski was not confirmed in the rank of brigadier general because several senators were unable to pronounce his name.

*T*he last Confederate troops to surrender were those of Surgeon Maj. Aaron P. Brown, of the Georgia State Line, who operated a field hospital in Upson County, Georgia, until captured on 23 August 1865.

★ ★ ★

*O*f nearly 360,000 Union war dead, almost 40 percent lie in graves marked "unknown" and 12 percent lie in unknown graves.

After the War

On their deaths Lt. Gen. Thomas "Stonewall" Jackson—who crossed the river on 10 May 1863—and Gen. Robert E. Lee—who followed on 12 October 1870—must both have immediately gone into action in Valhalla, for among the former's last words were apparently, "Order A.P. Hill to prepare for action," while the latter's included, "Tell A.P. Hill he must come up."—Hill himself had been killed in action 2 April 1865.

Although bureaucracies are noted for such things as "procedural errors" and "administrative oversights," it is nevertheless still remarkable that the famed U.S.S. *Monitor,* which went down in Force 7 winds off Cape Hatteras on 31 Dec 1862, was not officially declared "out of commission" by the U.S. Navy until nearly 91 years later, on 30 Sept. 1951.

★ ★ ★

*I*n the years after the Civil War the removal of the dangerous obstacles blocking the Hell Gate entry into New York Harbor—a task which required 125 tons of explosives—was supervised by John Newton, then chief of engineers, who was ably assisted by Mansfield Lovell, both men having previously served as major generals during the war, one on each side.

*F*rom time to time after the war Union Maj. Gen. Daniel Sickles, was wont to visit his leg, which, after having been amputated at Gettysburg, had been put on exhibit in the Army Medical Museum, where it may still be seen.

*H*enry H. Lockwood has an unusual burial place for a West Point graduate and brigadier general, for he lies at the United States Naval Academy in Annapolis, where he taught mathematics for many years both before and after the Civil War.

*S*enator John Sherman, who sponsored the famed Sherman Antitrust Act, had an older brother who was distinguished in a different line of work.

*I*n 1987 the remains of Confederate Maj. John D. Walker were stolen from a cemetery in Augusta, Georgia, resulting in a police investigation which lasted well into 1988, when a teenage student was arrested for what appears to have been a college prank.

*B*rig. Gen. Joseph K. Barnes, the surgeon general who pronounced President Abraham Lincoln dead in 1865, did the same for President James A. Garfield in 1881, thus becoming the only person ever to have attended the deathbed of two presidents.

*T*he Freedman's Bureau, organized to help former slaves adjust to freedom, fed millions of poor whites as well.

*T*he most controversial war bride of the Civil War was probably Miss Eleanor Swain, the daughter of Dr. David Swain, president of the University of North Carolina, who married Union brevet Brig. Gen. Smith D. Atkins while the latter was on occupation duty, touching off a storm of protest in the South which was so great that her father lost his job and she was never afterwards welcome in her hometown.

*I*n the 50 years after the war a score of men came forward each claiming to be John Wilkes Booth, and each with a different explanation for his survival.

*D*espite the fact that both his grandfather and father had died of wounds received in the military service of the United States, John Henry Hobart Ward survived both the Mexican War and the Civil War, rising from private to brigadier general, not giving up the ghost until 1903, when, 10 days after his 80th birthday, he was struck by a train.

*T*he Civil War provided the first two presidents from West Point, Jefferson Davis of the Confederate States and Ulysses S. Grant of the United States, who have been followed by Dwight D. Eisenhower of the United States and Anastasio Somoza of Nicaragua, in Central America.

★ ★ ★

*A*t the dedication of the Army and Navy Club in Washington in 1912, Civil War veteran and former club president Maj Gen. Charles F. Humphrey, who arrived in style, uniformed and mounted, rode his horse right up the front steps and into the bar, where he joined fellow members for several pitchers of daiquiris.

★ ★ ★

*B*y 1893 Civil War pension costs had risen to $193,000,000 a year.

★ ★ ★

*T*he first service medal authorized for award to United States military personnel was the Army Civil War Medal on 11 January 1905, which has a 1.25-inch medal showing Lincoln on the obverse pendant from a blue and gray ribbon; the Navy and Marine version, authorized 27 June 1908, shows the *Monitor-Merrimac* battle.

★ ★ ★

*T*he last surviving Civil War general was Union Brig. Gen. Adalbert Ames, who "crossed the river" in 1933 at the age of 97 years, five months, and 14 days.

★ ★ ★

*A*ccording to legend, when, not long after the war, a black man entered a Virginia church and knelt at the rail to receive communion, the first member of the all-white congregation to join him was Robert E. Lee.

As of 1 October 1986, 125 years after Ft. Sumter, Federal pensions were being paid to 14 wives of Civil War veterans—all of whom had been involved in May-December marriages in the early part of this century—including the widows of former Confederate veterans, eligible under an act of 1959, who were in some cases also collecting pensions from states of the *soi disant* Confederacy; another 64 pensions were being paid to surviving children of Civil War veterans.

★ ★ ★

In 1870 former Confederate Maj. Gen. Camille Armand Jules Marie, the Prince de Polignac, volunteered for service in the Franco-Prussian War, commanding a division with some skill and earning the Legion of Honor.

★ ★ ★

The Brooklyn tower of the Verrazano-Narrows Bridge rests on a reef formerly occupied by Fort Lafayette, used as a military prison during the Civil War.

★ ★ ★

A reenactment of the battle of Gettysburg held in June of 1988 involved some 10,000 uniformed participants, probably the largest concentration of boys in blue and boys in gray since the G.A.R. and the U.C.V. stopped holding mass joint reunions, over a half century earlier.

★ ★ ★

*I*n the 20 years after the Civil War the divorce rate in the nation increased 150 percent.

★ ★ ★

*L*earning that the war was over, some 500 Confederate soldiers at San Antonio confiscated about $80,000 in Confederate government silver and divided it among themselves, netting a cool $160 apiece and making them the only Confederate soldiers to receive mustering out pay at the end of the war.

★ ★ ★

*F*riedrich Karl von Schirach, who migrated to America shortly before the Civil War, had an honorable career in the Union Army, rising to the rank of brevet major, and later returning to his native Germany where he died within 10 days of the outbreak of war with the United States in 1917, by which time he had a grandson named Baldur von Schirach, who became the head of the Hitler Youth in a later war.

★ ★ ★

*C*onfederate Gen. Joseph E. Johnston died on 21 March 1891, apparently due to complications from a cold contracted six weeks earlier while standing bareheaded at the funeral of his good friend and erstwhile foe Gen. William T. Sherman.

The last Civil War veteran on active duty was John Lincoln Clem, who had signed up as a drummer boy in 1861 and retired as a major general in 1916.

★ ★ ★

The statue of Secretary of State William H. Seward which stands in Madison Square in New York City, has a head which is too small for its body, because when the memorial committee found itself short of funds, the sculptor gave them a bargain, placing Seward's head on a Lincoln torso which he had failed to sell: as a result, Lincoln holding the Emancipation Proclamation is now Seward holding the Alaska Purchase Treaty.

★ ★ ★

U.S. Grant's memoirs, completed shortly before his death in 1885 and published by his friend Mark Twain, earned $450,000 in royalties.

★ ★ ★

William Mack Lee, a former slave who was Robert E. Lee's personal body servant throughout the war, was born in 1838 and died in the early 1930s, by which time he had become a fixture at Confederate reunions.

★ ★ ★

*T*he indecisiveness of George Boulanger, who mismanaged an attempt to overthrow the French Republic in 1886, was first clearly demonstrated during the Civil War; he considered entering Federal service when the war broke out, but could never quite make up his mind, so that as late as January of 1865 he was still making inquiries.

★ ★ ★

*W*alter W. Williams, a Texan who died in 1960 at the alleged age of 118, is popularly regarded as the "last survivor of the Civil War," a distinction which in fact cannot be determined.

★ ★ ★

*B*y 1866 the national debt of the United States was $2,716,581,536.00, or $87.22 per capita: only Britain owed more money and only Britain, the Netherlands, and Hamburg had a higher per capita debt.

★ ★ ★

*G*racie Mansion, the home of the mayor of the city of New York, was formerly the home of the Gracie family, whose most distinguished Civil War connection was Confederate Brig. Gen. Archibald Gracie.

*A*rthur James Lyon Fremantle, a British guardsman who rose to become a lieutenant general and knight of the realm, was never under fire during his entire career save for the three days of Gettysburg, while he was visiting the Army of Northern Virginia, and once or twice during the brief Egyptian campaign of 1882.

★ ★ ★

*T*he first major motion picture was *The Birth of a Nation,* directed by D.W. Griffith, whose father had commanded a regiment in gray, a spectacular cinematic treatment of the Civil War and Reconstruction which had a so patently racist message that it led to a major revival of the Ku Klux Klan.

★ ★ ★

*T*he house at Mt. McGregor, New York, in which Ulysses S. Grant spent his last days writing his memoirs while dying of cancer, now lies in the middle of a so-called "correctional institution."

★ ★ ★

*T*he *201st Infantry,* an element of the West Virginia National Guard, has what is perhaps the most unique distinction of any military unit in history; because its ancestral Virginia militia regiment split at the start of the Civil War, it has battle streamers for both Union and Confederate service, each of which includes the second battle of Bull Run, at which, in effect, the regiment fought itself.

*O*f the 330 Confederate generals who did not die while in the service, 8 died in "personal encounters" of one sort or another, 4 of them in Mississippi.

*W*hen serving as the American military observer with the Prussian Army during the Franco-Prussian War (1870-1871), Lt. Gen. Philip Sheridan was asked by a high Prussian officer—very possibly the great Helmuth von Moltke himself—how he thought the United States Army would do against the Prussians, to which he replied, "Grant, if given the armies of the Potomac and the Tennessee, would land in Lisbon and capture Berlin in six weeks."

*B*y testamentary request, "The Battle Hymn of the Republic" was sung at the funeral of Sir Winston S. Churchill in Westminster Abbey.

*M*argaret Mitchell, author of *Gone with the Wind*, was the granddaughter of First Sergeant Russel C. Mitchell, of *Company I, 1st Texas Infantry*, in Hood's Texas Brigade of the Army of Northern Virginia.

★ ★ ★

*A*mong the guests present when the restored McLean House at Appomattox was dedicated as a museum in 1950 were Ulysses S. Grant III and Robert E. Lee IV, the namesakes of two gentlemen who had once had occasion to meet in the McLean parlor.

★ ★ ★

*O*bserving the equestrian statue of Sherman being guided by Victory which stands at the foot of Central Park, a Southern belle is said to have re-marked, "Just like a Yankee, to let a lady walk."

★ ★ ★

*A*t demonstrations in 1987 in Arcadia, Florida, which resulted in the burning of the home of two young hemophiliacs infected with the AIDS virus, the Confederate battle flag was prominently displayed both by the rioters and the father of the boys in question.

★ ★ ★

*E*rroll Flynn, who made a number of films loosely based on the Civil War, played George Armstrong Custer in *They Died with Their Boots On* (1941), during which he attacked J.E.B. Stuart, whom he had played in *Santa Fe Trail* (1940), in which Custer was played by a third-rate actor who later moved to Washington.

*W*hen someone observed that although he had taken part in some 63 battles and skirmishes during the war he had not once been wounded, former Confederate Brig. Gen. Reuben L. Walker replied, "It was not my fault."

*T*he first commissioner of baseball was Judge Kennesaw Mountain Landis of Illinois, who was named after the battle in which his father had been wounded in 1864.

*W*hile in France on his world tour after leaving the Presidency, Ulysses S. Grant was asked what he had learned from Napoleon, to which he replied, "I faced two problems during the war. One was the rifled musket behind works and the other was moving huge amounts of men and material by rail. Napoleon had nothing to say on either of them."

*T*he only Justice of the United States Supreme Court to have ever been a prisoner-of-war was Edward D. White of Louisiana, who was named to the post in 1894, little more than 30 years after he had been bagged at Vicksburg while fighting for the Confederacy.

*N*ot until World War II did the United States Army realize it was no longer necessary for soldiers to have perfect teeth in order to bite their cartridges, at which point a large number of men with malocclusions suddenly became I-A.

*O*n 5 April 1917, former Corp. Henry Lewis and former Pvt. Henry Peters of the erstwhile *Company B, 47th Ohio* were awarded the Medal of Honor for heroism at Vicksburg, 53 years, 11 months, and two days before, thus becoming the last Civil War winners of the highest decoration.

*I*n 1867 Robert E. Lee declined the dubious distinction of becoming the first "Grand Wizard" of the recently formed Ku Klux Klan, a post which was then assumed by the notorious racist Nathan Bedford Forrest.

Samuel Powhatan Carter is the only American officer ever to rank as both a general and an admiral: an Annapolis graduate and naval officer, he was seconded to the Volunteer Army during the war, rising to brigadier general and brevet major general, and when peace came reverted to the navy and rose to rear admiral.

During the storming of San Juan Hill, outside of Santiago de Cuba in 1898, Maj. Gen. Joseph Wheeler, a retread Confederate, allegedly cried, "We've got them damn Yankees on the run!"

The first novel to be adapted for the screen was *Ben Hur: A Tale of the Christ* by former Union Maj. Gen. Lew Wallace.

In 1972 the United States Naval Ordnance School issued a special manual on Civil War ammunition to assist in the disposal of the untold thousands of unexploded rounds which still can be found on many of the old battlefields.

Shortly before World War I an enterprising capitalist obtained 100,000 Civil War-era glass photographic plate negatives, which he processed for the silver and glass content.

Since its first publication in 1936 Margaret Mitchell's *Gone with the Wind* has sold over 28,000,000 copies, more than all other books on the Civil War combined.

★ ★ ★

Many of the charts used by the United States Navy during operations in the Pacific in World War II were copies of those made by the United States Exploring Expedition, which had conducted the only scientific survey of several areas, in 1838-1842, under the direction of Lt. Charles Wilkes, who gained fame in the Civil War as a result of the *Trent Affair*.

★ ★ ★

When the *15th New York National Guard*—a black outfit which later became the *369th Infan*try— was organized shortly before World War I, its recruiting surgeon was Dr. George Bolling Lee, "whose grandfather had given up the military persuasion at Appomattox."

★ ★ ★

The Confederate battleflag which flew over the casket of Gen. Pierre G.T. Beauregard in 1893 was that which he had been given by the vivacious Jennie Cary girls in 1861.

*I*n 1987 a crowd of more than 40,000 sight-seers watched some 6,000 men reenact the battle of Shiloh, the total number of people present being greater than that of Confederate troops back in 1862.

★ ★ ★

*B*rig. Gen. Nathan Bedford Forrest, the grandson of the Confederate cavalryman, died in 1943 while on a bombing mission over Germany.

★ ★ ★

*N*early 125 years after the Civil War, only North Carolina among the former Confederate states observes Lincoln's birthday as a holiday; while Alabama and Mississippi celebrate both Davis' and Lee's birthdays, Virginia has a Lee-Jackson Day, Texas a Confederate Heroes Day, and Mississippi a Confederate Memorial Day; on the other hand, all of the former Confederate States observe Martin Luther King's birthday.

★ ★ ★

*F*or many years after the Civil War former Confederate Pvt. Benjamin Thorpe of the 26th North Carolina arranged for flowers to be placed every Memorial Day on the grave of Union Maj. Gen. John F. Reynolds, whom he claimed to have killed while serving as a sniper on the first day of the battle of Gettysburg.

*M*ore Civil War generals are associated in death with New York City than any other place in the nation: of 425 Confederate generals, 4 died and are buried there, 12 died there and are buried elsewhere, and 4 died elsewhere and are buried there, for a total of 20 (4.7 percent); while of 583 Union generals, 25 died and are buried there, 43 died there and are buried elsewhere, and 10 died elsewhere but are buried there, for a total of 78 (13.3 percent).

★ ★ ★

*T*he Confederate battle flag forms the principal charge of the state flags of Georgia and Mississippi.

★ ★ ★

*T*he highest government post ever attained by a Confedcrate veteran was that of chief justice of the Supreme Court, held by Edward D. White of Louisiana, from 1910 until his death in 1921, by which time he had served 26 years on the high court; White also has the dubious distinction of being the highest ranking government official to have been a member of the Ku Klux Klan.

★ ★ ★

*B*y 1906 Federal expenditures on Civil War veterans' benefits totaled $3,300,000,000, more than half the $6,190,000,000 which the war and subsequent occupation of the South had cost.

*I*t is said that when, shortly after the war, Lt. Gen. Ulysses S. Grant, commander of the finest army in the world, winner of scores of battles, conqueror of the Confederacy, and rumored presidential candidate, paid a visit to his aged parents, his mother greeted him by saying, "Well, Ulysses, you've become a great man, haven't you?" and then went back to her housework.

★ ★ ★

*I*n the 130 years since the Civil War, over 5,000 black people have been lynched in the United States.

★ ★ ★

*A*rguably the most amusing work ever written about the Civil War is Thomas Connelly's "That Was the War that Was," which appeared in *The Journal of Mississippi History* in 1968, although Karl Marx's and Frederick Engels' *The Civil War in the United States* (New York, 1937) is almost as funny for different reasons.

★ ★ ★

*O*ne beneficial side effect of the elimination of horses from armies is that troops are no longer susceptible to mange, glanders, or any of several other equine diseases which can infect people.

*B*rig. Gen. Alexander S. Webb, who won a Medal of Honor for the defense of The Angle at Gettysburg on 3 July 1863, went on to serve with considerable distinction as the president of the City College of New York from 1869 through 1902.

★ ★ ★

*W*hile only one of the 583 Union generals died in a so-called "personal encounter," fully 11 of 425 Confederate generals did, three during the war and 8 after it.

★ ★ ★

*O*n 21 June 1987 a reenactment of the battle of Glorieta Pass, New Mexico, attracted some 4,000 spectators, who not only greatly outnumbered the reenactors, but also outnumbered the combined total of 2,500 men who actually fought there in 1862.

★ ★ ★

*W*hen criticized for alleged errors in his memoirs, William T. Sherman replied, "I may be wrong, but that's the way I remembered it. These are my memoirs, not the memoirs of anybody else."

★ ★ ★

*T*o the great annoyance of the black citizens of the state, a Confederate flag still flies from the Alabama state capitol.